Reflective Practices:
Perspectives of Multi-Unicultural
School Leaders

Dr. Paul A. Rodríguez

Dr. Roberto F. Casas

Copyright © 2016

Cogito Consulting, LLC

Dr. Paul A. Rodríguez

Dr. Roberto F. Casas

All rights reserved.

ISBN-10:0-9863065-5-X
ISBN-13: 978-0-9863065-5-6

DEDICATION

For my children, Paul, Alex and Harmonie, grandchildren Elijah, Luna, Carson and Maggie. May they develop knowledge and continued interest in education, philosophy and music. For Doreen, who has supported me in all my endeavors.

For Hilda Padilla-Casas, for her years of support of all my educational endeavors, Dedicate to my parents: Frank L. Casas and Esperanza Esther Casas, Brother Ernesto (a.k.a.Shaverz) and sister Martha RIP.

CONTENTS

	Dedication	Iii
	Acknowledgments	viii
1	CHAPTER	1
	Introduction	
2	CHAPTER	13
	Reflective Daily Leadership and Ethical Actions	
3	CHAPTER	28
	Conceptual Frameworks through Reflection	

*Reflective Practices:
Perspectives of Multi-Unicultural School
Leaders*

| 4 | CHAPTER | 51 |

Guidelines for Engaging in
Reflective Practice

| 5 | CHAPTER | 55 |

QUALITITES OF EFFECTIVE
LEADERSHIP: PRINCIPLES
OF PETER F. Drucker

| 6 | CHAPTER | 82 |

Reflection on a Leadership-
Value System

| 7 | CHAPTER | 96 |

Leaders Must Adapt through
Change with Restraint

Dr. Paul A. Rodríguez & Dr. Roberto F. Casas

8	CHAPTER	96

Vail High School: A Mosaic of Backgrounds for Change

9	CHAPTER	116

A Multi-unicultural Reflection: Music and the Arts

10	CHAPTER	158

California Common Core Standards: Concerns/ Considerations for Alternative Education Students, Schools, and Programs

11	CHAPTER	176

An Alternative Instructional Delivery Model: The Independent Study Program

Reflective Practices:
Perspectives of Multi-Unicultural School
Leaders

References 211

About the Authors 223

ACKNOWLEDGMENTS

For my parents, Maria Fernández Rodriguez (R.I.P. 1991) and Salvador Zuñiga Rodriguez (R.I.P. 1992).

For my sons, stepchildren and grandchildren (Phoebe, Lynessa, John, Andrew, Isaac and Albert, Jr,).

Sherman Garnett: The first Principal of the Chaffey Community Schools and lessons learned from him.

Dr. Preston Carr for his continuous support, all the family on the Pascua Yaqui Tribe Reservation, Tucson Arizona. Sister Olivia O. Casas-Lux, friends, family, professional colleagues and car club members.

x

CHAPTER 1
INTRODUCTION

We have written this book because of our unique and real concern for improving education for children who are "at risk" of school failure. Whether these students are of different ethnicities or speak different languages, the students are not failures, but have difficulty maneuvering in a system we call school. In order to improve education, we have to improve schools and the practices of school leaders. This transformation of schools requires change and improvement of individuals in school leadership positions. In order to change school leaders and their practices toward improvement, we must replicate what is working for kids through reflective practice. Osterman and Kottkamp (1993) offered this perspective:

Dr. Paul A. Rodríguez & Dr. Roberto F. Casas

We believe that reflective practice, an approach to educational improvement that is both situational and places the professional in the very center of the attempt to create improvement not only stands in contrast to most other current ideas but has the greatest potential of any approach improving individuals and, through them, schools and education. (p. vii).

The book was written because we share professional practices and intellectual interests in reflection and reflective practice. We are passionate that reflection has the best hope and significant change in how leaders examine their personal beliefs, values, and behaviors in such a way that members of the school community realize that it is they who must adapt their

***Reflective Practices:
Perspectives of Multi-Unicultural School
Leaders***

practices to meet the needs of students at risk and the diverse communities they serve. However, before we discuss the importance of reflective practice, we need to arrive at a definition of reflective practice. Schon (1983) defines reflective practice as "the capacity to reflect on action so as to engage in a process of continuous learning." Similarly, Bolton (2010) stated that reflective practice involves "playing critical attention to practical values and theories which inform everyday action, by examining practice reflectively and reflexively. This leads to developmental insight." Another idea by Boud et al. (1985) states, "Reflection is an important human activity in which people recapture their experience, think about it, mull it over and evaluate it. It is this working with experience that is important in learning." As for education, Larrivee (2000) argues,

Dr. Paul A. Rodríguez & Dr. Roberto F. Casas

"Reflective practice refers to the process of the educator studying his or her own teaching methods and determining what works best for students. It involves the consideration of the ethical consequences of classroom procedures on students."

Training Future Reflective School Leaders

Reflective practice has been our mantra of ensuring that future leaders of diverse students, including English language learners and other at-risk students, are reflective, culturally proficient educators. Reflective practice helps us discover the link between theory and our professing and stressing our professional practice and between professing and transformational personal action to improve the quality of public schools. We are true believers of this practice because it leads to cultural competency and proficiency.

Reflective Practices: Perspectives of Multi-Unicultural School Leaders

Lindsey, Nuri Robbins, and Terrell (2002) asserted,

> Cultural proficiency is an inside-out perspective on change in which leaders transform approaches to their personal leadership behaviors and school practices. Leaders who manifest cultural proficiency guide their colleagues to examine personal values and a behavior in such a way that members of schools realize that is they who must adapt their practices to meet the needs of their students and community they serve. (p. 2)

Albeit, reflection and reflective practice have become common buzzwords, we believe it can assist leaders and others to examine and evaluate how schools develop, implement, and enforce policies and practices that represent its position on issues of diversity.

Reflection for School Improvement

Dr. Paul A. Rodríguez & Dr. Roberto F. Casas

The purpose in writing this book is to help school leaders reflect on their own practices and who are committed to improving the educational quality of schools and who want to improve their own professional development and practices. Leaders in schools with diverse student populations, who choose to incorporate reflective practices in their daily leadership (introspection), will develop more effective administrative skills. Illuminating Griffith's (1979) idea "that educating must be grounded in the ordinary experiences of individual people and expressed in ordinary language; we have attempted to explain conceptual terms in simple language and to illustrate these concepts using examples drawn from everyday experiences."

    Writing about our reflections and our approaches toward successful practices that impact teaching and learning has forced us to clarify conceptual issues and to confront and define problems that were somewhat vague before we began. We

Reflective Practices:
Perspectives of Multi-Unicultural School Leaders

have learned a great deal as "minority" school administrators in regards to navigating through the "political waters" in educating our diverse student population. We have gleaned ideas and practices from other ethnical and diverse school leaders by utilizing reflection to narrow the achievement gap of our at-risk students. I hope that we can save our readers time and frustration by sharing our reflections/introspections and what has been learned in the field. Deal and Peterson (1999) provide this opinion: "With all evidence from both business and education highlighting culture as a critical aspect of organizational cohesion and performance, what's holding us back? Why do standards and restructuring continue to play such dominant role in educational improvement and reform? Part of the explanation lies in the way we look at educational organizations" (p. 9).

Dr. Paul A. Rodríguez & Dr. Roberto F. Casas

Practical Experiences and Personal Successes

This is not a book about traditional educational theory, but on practical experiences and personal successes and failures. It has required us to roll up our sleeves and to interact with ethnically diverse educators of at-risk students and how they helped students go from "at risk" to "at promise." These leaders discuss their years of experiences and practices and fine tuning their modus operandi through reflective practice. Through the leadership of the principal, Dr. Paul Rodriguez, Vail High School (an alternative school in the Montebello Unified School District) was able to reflect on practices and organizational change that would eventually earn the school the designation of "a California distinguished school." Several reflective practices that were applied by Dr. Rodriguez toward systematic change were adopted at Vail High School, a continuation high school in Montebello Unified School

***Reflective Practices:
Perspectives of Multi-Unicultural School
Leaders***

District, east of Los Angeles in Southern California.

Overview

On a daily basis, we think about our leadership and the impact on the ongoing operations of our schools. We are firm believers in the art of reflective practice. Reflective practice provides an informal evaluation and assessment toward improvement of our educational functions. Reflective practice frames the process of continuous improvement. It addresses questions about leadership, authority, and one's own upbringing and how we tackle hard problems. Reflective practice helps us to adjust, fine-tune, and change the way we do business through daily experiences and real-life situations. Reflective practices have a direct impact on our leadership style. It helps us to recognize conflicts over values and establish purpose. Reflective leaders in high-performing schools

Dr. Paul A. Rodríguez & Dr. Roberto F. Casas

"recognize and utilize the cultural, ethnic, racial, and economic diversity of the school community to meet the needs of all learners and to maximize the performance of students" (Wallace Foundation's Leadership Effectiveness Knowledge Foundation Exploration Committee, 2004, p. 11).

Leadership requires various learning strategies and relies on complex, organic, interpersonal relationships between leaders and followers. With this in mind, we have developed some practical ideas, reflections, and thoughts about the practice of reflective leadership. These initiatives will help us to develop the various chapters of this book.

Reflective leadership takes place every day.
Reflective leadership helps us develop conceptual frameworks for practice.
Reflective leadership provides the ability to effect change even through adversity.

Reflective Practices:
Perspectives of Multi-Unicultural School
Leaders

Reflection helps us develop our values, which play a key role in the development of authority and leadership styles.

Reflective leadership conjures up images of social contract—the ability to mobilize and develop our own focus.

Reflective leadership helps in the contingency theory where a leader earns influence by adapting to various situations.

Leaders, through reflective practice, develop values systems. People with competing values engage one another as they confront a shared situation from their own point of view.

Reflective leadership is setting the frame, establishing the bottom line, making unpopular decisions.

Leadership through reflection provides the ability to adapt by using restraint.

Reflection helps leaders in dealing with tough realities.

Leadership through reflection means having a clear vision and the capacity to

persuade people to move in a positive and forward direction.
The anguish of leadership is derived through reflection by what we learn through experiences.
Leadership oftentimes is a passionate and consuming activity; the practice of leadership requires reflection for a sense of purpose.

Thus, reflective practice cannot be used to maintain the status quo. Leadership, as it relates to reflective practice, helps us to learn that only by changing ourselves do we have the ability to change and lead others or the course of direction.
Leadership, say Heifetz and Linsky (2002), is "about getting more out of life by putting more into it" and "putting yourself and your ideas on the line, responding effectively to risks, and living to celebrate the meaning of you efforts" (p. 3). Fullan (2003) states, "These days doing nothing as a leader is a great risk, so you might as well take risks worth taking" (p. 63).

CHAPTER 2
Reflective Daily Leadership and Ethical Actions

This book is about leadership with the school principal/leader and the "reflective practitioner" as the focus. Preparing to lead a school site on a daily basis is no small task. Some leadership actions are planned and scripted, while other actions are situational and prioritized based on the circumstances at hand. The outcome of each situation is based on reflection and past experiences. Our values, cultural upbringing, as well as reflection, play an important role in our decision-making. According to Heifetz (1994), "leadership involves our self-images and moral codes." Heifetz further asserts that "we cannot talk about leadership and then say leadership is value free" (p. 14).

As minority school leaders, we bring our cultural, ethnic pride, personal and professional values to each situation or

Dr. Paul A. Rodríguez & Dr. Roberto F. Casas

matter. Some of us look at situations from two lenses. There were times in my years as a site principal where I would reflect on past personal and professional experience to situations and would ask myself, "What would my abuelita (grandmother) do in this situation?" Often times, I could hear her voice advising me in Spanish and reflecting on the consequences of my actions. Thinking back on her advice, the cultural and heritage realm comes into play. She would always implore us "to do what was morally right." However, as a site principal (in the heat of the moment), I would ask myself, "Do I do what is right, or do I do the right thing?" How I responded to situations often determined the school culture. Deal and Peterson (1999) asserts, "When school leaders have reflected and feel they understand a school culture, they can evaluate the need to shape or reinforce it. Valuable aspects of the school's existing culture can be reinforced, problematic ones revitalized, and toxic ones given strong antidotes" (p. 87). As minority school

Reflective Practices:
Perspectives of Multi-Unicultural School
Leaders

leaders, we must recognize that ethnic pride among our parents, students, and communities is a key factor for our students' success. Daggett and Kruse (1997) expound that ethnic pride is a strong motivator.

It also has to be recognized that a big stick, by itself, will not do the job. Curricula at schools serving ethnic minorities are going to have to be altered to include content that encourages students to be proud of who they are and where they come from. All minorities have made positive, strong contributions to the growth and strength of America—contributions about which current generations have a right to be informed and to display just pride. Unquestionably, distorted views of American history have deprived minorities of these perspectives in the past. That is going to have to change. Progress toward establishing a real-world perspective in education is going to have to encompass a mutual recognition of the diversity that is America and the values o f the diverse parts of the complex makeup of the population. (p. 316)

School culture/climate affects every part of the school enterprise from parental choice, flexibility, instruction, and staff involvement. Often times, school culture will have positive or negative effects on teaching and learning. Test scores are often a by-product of school climate. When I reflected on my processes to solve site-level problems utilizing reflective practices, what would emerge was a school environment where teachers had time to plan and practice, students had time to ponder, and parents had time to participate. Osterman and Kottkamp (1993) stated the following:

Reflective practice is potentially powerful avenue for school involvement and systematic change. We say "potentially" because it has not been tried yet in any serious way. To try seriously means calling off "business as usual" and trusting

Reflective Practices:
Perspectives of Multi-Unicultural School Leaders

professional educators and parents in ways not even considered under many contemporary reform proposals and our pervasive, "usual" Modal I way of doing things. To try it seriously means accepting on a broad front the kinds of beliefs and attitudes we recommended for facilitators. (p. 187)

Most school cultures are stable, but not static, and changes do occur. School leaders can play major roles in acknowledging these transitions and recognize the pain of transitions by designing events that make transitions a collective experience, healing whatever wounds they create and helping the school/district adapt to change in terms of its traditions and culture. Symbolic leadership is needed when schools are new or when they require considerable transformation to serve their students. On a daily basis, school leaders face many difficult challenges in meeting the diverse needs of their school communities. Reinhartz and Beach (2004) stated, "As leaders negotiate through the complex and quickly changing circumstances that occur in schools, they must make decisions not only for the good of each student, but they must also consider the good of the campus and district as well." As leaders function within organizations, most have established a set of values and principles that shapes and guides their behaviors based on reflective practice. The American Association of School Administrators has adopted a code of ethics that serves to guide school leaders and mold their behaviors. The code seems idealistic, but is practical because it applies to school leaders in a variety of roles and venues. Albeit the administrators' code of ethics has been adopted well over two decades, some school leaders may not be privy to the specific behaviors identified in the document. School leaders should not only be aware of the Code of Ethics for

Reflective Practices:
Perspectives of Multi-Unicultural School Leaders

Administrators, but should integrate them into their daily routines.

TABLE 1.1 Codes of Ethics for Administrators

Make the well being of students the fundamental value of all decision-making and actions

Fulfills professional responsibilities with honesty and integrity

Supports the principle of due process and protects the civil and human rights of all individuals

Obeys local, state and national laws and does not knowingly join or support organizations that advocate, directly or indirectly, the overthrow of the government

Implements the governing board of education's policies and administrative rules and regulations

Pursues appropriate measures to correct those laws, policies, and regulations that are not consistent with sound educational goals

Avoids using positions for personal gain through political, social, religious, economic, or other influences

Accepts academic degrees or professional certifications only from accredited institutions

Maintains the standards and seeks to improve the effectiveness of the profession through research and continuing professional development

Honors all contracts until fulfillment, release, or dissolution mutually agreed upon by all parties to contract

Source: Adopted by American Association of School Administrators Executive Committee, 1981—American Association of School Administrators.

Adams and Maine (1998) suggest that an understanding of ethics provides a way to confront issues, understand complexities of a situation, consider options to problem solving, and search for a solution. The

Reflective Practices:
Perspectives of Multi-Unicultural School Leaders

solution must be equitable and fair and meet the many guideline parameters of ethical conduct.

How do school leaders make fair and appropriate decisions that reflect ethical behavior? Blanchard and Peale (1998) offer the following questions that provide a quick ethics check. When confronted with an ethical decision, the leader should ask the following:
Is it legal?
Is it balanced?
How will it make me feel about myself? (p. 27)

In answering these questions, school leaders must first decide if their behavior will violate state or federal statutes or mandates, education codes, or school policy. Further, they must determine if their actions are fair to all parties, making sure that they are not "arbitrary and capricious." Finally, leaders must ask themselves if they can live in peace with their decisions and actions. Would they be able to "look in the mirror" if their decisions were the focus of a newspaper editorial or the evening news?

We Are Marshall

When Principal Carlos Hernandez was asked to open and develop a brand-new school in the Lynwood Unified School District, he reflected on this transformation. The school was named Thurgood Marshall Elementary School. It was still a semester away from opening its doors to the first group of students. Students and families resided in different neighborhoods in the city of Lynwood, and the redrawing of school boundaries brought a unique group of children together. Carlos, in his quest to bring immediate culture to the school, started reflecting on what the school mascot should be, what the school colors should be, and similar thoughts. He remembered that his favorite professional football player, Randy Moss (playing for the

Reflective Practices:
Perspectives of Multi-Unicultural School
Leaders

Oakland Raiders), attended Marshall University in West Virginia. Carlos then thought, "What if I contacted Marshall University to see if they can develop a partnership with Marshall Elementary School?"

The results of Carlos's reflections were that John Marshall University allowed Thurgood Marshall Elementary School to use their school colors of green, white, and black. Although Marshall University's mascot is a buffalo and their sports teams are referred to as the Thundering Herd, Marshall Elementary became the Stampede, utilizing a baby buffalo as its mascot. What developed from Mr. Hernandez's reflections was a partnership that developed into a professional teaching community where research, professional development, and trainings were shared via virtual and distance learning television between both Marshall schools. Marshall Elementary fifth grade students and teachers were invited

Dr. Paul A. Rodríguez & Dr. Roberto F. Casas

and visited Marshall University in West Virginia. The video conferencing aspect allowed Marshall Elementary and Marshall University to share ideas, provide professional development, and to share cultural activities with several elementary schools in West Virginia. Music assemblies were scheduled by Marshall Elementary School with the Los Angeles Music Center providing musical groups and styles from different parts of the world. Students in West Virginia were able to participate in the concerts and view the assemblies through video conferencing. Carlos Hernandez, as well as the provost and others from Marshall University, developed a professional learning community (PLC), making presentations on their partnership at the National PLC Conferences in Orlando, Florida, and Las Vegas, Nevada.

In a telephone interview with Carlos Hernandez (personal communication, March 10, 2011), he added the following information about the results of his

Reflective Practices:
Perspectives of Multi-Unicultural School
Leaders

reflections as to other key points of Marshall Elementary school climate:

The partnership between Marshall Elementary School and Marshall University opened doors that students and parents thought were closed.
The partnership brought the East Coast to Marshall Elementary and the West Coast to the elementary schools that were partnered with Marshall University in West Virginia through video conferencing and through the visits to Marshall University.
The partnership broadened our students' perspective about culture.
The partnership created an environment unlike any other district school.
There was pride of ownership with students, parents, and teachers.
The teachers' perspectives about the students changed. Some teachers had the same students at Roosevelt Elementary School the year prior, but saw the students differently at Marshall Elementary since the

overall school's attitude was different; this was better in Marshall's case.
Marshall Elementary School stood out because the culture of the school was welcoming and nurturing.
The students expectations were raised; we were not going to do anything the way they were used to do things. Students knew that if they maintained good grades and attendance through the rest of middle and high school, they had the opportunity of attending Marshall University.
It took a while for parents to get used to the "Marshall" way, but the change was a positive one.
Overall, the Marshall Elementary School environment made it a desirable school for many parents and students in the city of Lynwood.

Strategies and Considerations

Reflective Practices:
Perspectives of Multi-Unicultural School Leaders

Principled and ethical-centered leadership is key in the development of authority. Having authority brings not only resources to bear, but also serious constraints on the exercise of leadership. We need to understand these resources and constraints. As leaders we must ask ourselves, are our decisions legal? Are they balanced? How will I feel about myself going forward?

CHAPTER 3
CONCEPTUAL FRAMEWORKS THROUGH REFLECTION

In the book, Shaping School Culture: The Heart of Leadership, the authors Terence Deal and Kent Peterson discuss the notion of beliefs as a way of beginning to frame the concepts of leadership. Deal and Peterson (1999) decreed the following:

Beliefs originate in-group and personal experiences and through reading books and articles. Beliefs are powerful in schools because they represent the core understandings about student capacity (immutable or alterable), teacher responsibility for learning (little or lot), expert sources of teacher knowledge (experience, research, or intuition), and educational success (will never happen or is achievable. (p. 27)

School leaders take on various symbolic roles in their practice. Once the school

Reflective Practices:
Perspectives of Multi-Unicultural School Leaders

leaders have reflected and believe they understand the school culture, they can assess and evaluate the need to shape it through personal, cultural, and professional experiences. Unique and valuable aspects of the school's current culture can be reinforced, problem areas can be renewed, and cancerous ones can be given strong doses of remedies. The public educational system in America must stay in step with change, and teachers must train students in using techniques and strategies to compete in the global marketplace. The global economy and financial structures will determine the process of change. Economic trends, corporate strategic plans, and the universal decision-making will affect education. Education delivery models must be on the cutting edge concerning technology used by students. No longer can students afford to participate in lockstep curriculum designs, but rather must obtain experiences that enable them to actively participate in microcorporations, team decision making, authentic assessment, portfolio building, and strategic planning.

Students must be encouraged to think globally and out of the box and use the community and the world as their learning environment through distance learning and by researching through the World Wide Web. Teachers must take on new professional roles and take on leadership functions. Teachers must be more than bearers of information must. Teachers must be risk takers, functioning with energy, maturity, and integrity. Reflective practice will allow principals and administrators the ability to empower teachers to dream, plan, and work in simultaneously structured and creative environments. Dr. Lorraine Monroe, author of the book Nothing is Impossible, addressed participants of the National Ed.D. Program for Educational Leaders Summer Institute in 2001 at Nova Southeastern University in Fort Lauderdale, Florida. She stated that school personnel

Reflective Practices:
Perspectives of Multi-Unicultural School
Leaders

should continue to do what is working and that teachers "must be a bit crazy and do crazy things for children" to help students realize their full potential (Monroe 1998).

An alternative educational school, known formerly as Chaffey West Community Day School, located in Ontario, California, had teachers who collaborated on a regular basis as to how to best serve students to enable them to be competitive and function in society. The county principal of Chaffey West Community Day School, which was one of many sites under the West End Community Day School system, was always reflecting on best practices and different ways of serving students. Because of his reflective leadership practices, he encouraged teachers to think "out of the box" on their instructional delivery. Chaffey West teacher and author, Mark Kennedy (1994), stated in his article, "The Ownership Project: An Experiment with Student Equity,"

Dr. Paul A. Rodríguez & Dr. Roberto F. Casas

The teacher controls class design, curriculum and assessment, student activities, resources and rules for behavior: in effect, which will learn, when and using what. Students are guests of the teacher, and in no way considered to have ownership-either by the teacher or themselves. (p. 24)

Chaffey West was one of fourteen classroom sites in the west end of San Bernardino County. The school cluster consisted of five classrooms, which served secondary-aged students in grades seven through twelve. The students were either expelled from their regular comprehensive district schools, on formal probation as juvenile offenders, or where considered at risk of dropping out of school because of non-school success. Many of the students were affiliated with the various gangs in the area served by Chaffey West. Teachers were encouraged and empowered to utilize instructional practices, which engaged and encouraged students to prepare for the new era.

Chaffey West consisted of teachers who were allowed and supported by their principal to serve in leadership roles for the San Bernardino County Superintendent of Schools office. Teachers served as lead teachers, mentor teachers, technology mentors, coordinators, and facilitators for the school accreditation process (WASC and PQR), presenters, and at national education conferences, as County Schools Steering Committee members, authors of articles and books, and they had the county teacher of the year on staff. This staff was passionate for their professional work and daily impact on students. The principal and teachers were driven by the desire to develop forward-thinking students. The principal empowered and encouraged teachers to provide optimal learning opportunities for students. The principal and author of this book, Roberto Casas,

Dr. Paul A. Rodríguez & Dr. Roberto F. Casas

describe examples of several instructional techniques and strategies that were practiced by Chaffey West teachers to enhance the core courses. They were as follows:

Microsociety

The society consisted of three basic segments. Segment 1 consisted of a city government (as the centerpiece), segment two as a county/state government (including a court system), and segment three as the private sector such as the microcorporations (the bank and newspaper). Students had to fill out job applications and go through an interview to hold various positions in the microcorporations. Students were paid for the quality and quantity of schoolwork accomplished. The students were paid in "team money" and were charged for student desk rental and other incidentals such as a pencil if they forgot theirs. Students earned salaries and could purchase items from the corporate store. Further, several vice presidents ran by a chief executive officer (CEO) as well as the classroom. Students could also serve in entry-level positions in the corporation. According to Kennedy (2001),

If we want students to take ownership in and responsibility for their own learning results by exploring, strengthening, and ultimately using their own perspectives, we have no choice but to set up systems that will give them the freedom to do so. A democratic classroom management model is such a system. (p. 88)

Chess as a Learning Tool

Chess is an interactive, authentic, three-dimensional activity that naturally encourages and supports marginalized students in successful transitions toward expanding their vision of the world beyond their home turf and toward academic proficiency and confidence. In addition, chess can help educators gain an understanding of what it means to be, and who is perceived to be, intelligent. These powerful benefits of introducing chess into schools and other youth settings make it clear in the classroom can be much more than just a game. (p. 19)

Chess was more than just a game learned by all students at Chaffey West. It was designed for the following:

Helping student's transition from a closed-turf mentality to an open, neighborly outlook.
Helping student's transition from disconnectedness to confidence in their abilities in at least one academic core area.
Helping teacher's transition from a narrow, traditional definition of intelligence to a wider, more inclusive understanding of what it means to be smart.

Reflective Practices:
Perspectives of Multi-Unicultural School
Leaders

Kennedy (1998) stated that when chess was included in the classroom, the three transitions above were evident in eight powerful ways:

Chess removes barriers between students.
Chess gives students at least one reason to come to school.
Chess builds rapport between adults and students.
Chess honors nontraditional cognitive styles.
Chess builds life skills and critical thinking / strategic planning.
Chess builds meta-cognition as students learn to examine their own thinking.
Chess integrates different types of thinking.
Chess challenges and expands our understanding of intelligence. (p. 19)

WIA Summer Youth Employment Program
Chaffey West teacher Mr. Donald English administered the Summer Youth

Dr. Paul A. Rodríguez & Dr. Roberto F. Casas

Employment Program in 2000. Mr. English was the San Bernardino County teacher of the year and was eager to provide employment opportunities to students of Chaffey West Community Day School. The WIA (Workforce Investment Act) Summer Youth Employment Program consisted of a grant funding of four hundred thousand dollars that provided for the employment of fifty students. Students received pre-employment work-maturity skills training as well as academic remedial skills training. The top student participant from the 1999 Summer Youth Employment Program was hired as part of the 2000 WIA staff to assist in monitoring work sites.

Another feature of this program was student participation in cultural awareness programs, team building activities, and community service. Activities included attendance at a Los Angeles Sparks basketball game, a camping retreat through the Boy Scouts of America, and participation in the Latin Sounds 2000

***Reflective Practices:
Perspectives of Multi-Unicultural School
Leaders***

MOVE (Music as an Opportunity to Vocational Enrichment) Program.

The MOVE program goals are as follows:

Provide educational enrichment activity designed to improve cross-cultural awareness of Latin music with special emphasis on African-Native New World, Old World, and Third World contributions.
Recognize the Summer Youth Employment Program participation and success through incentive and reward activity.
Incorporate Latin music appreciation, history theory, and practice in an innovative school-retention program.

Features and benefits:

Increase student self-esteem
Improve cross-cultural relations by identifying ethnic, national, and cultural contributions in Latin music.
Reward students for positive performance

Unlock untapped education and learning through teacher training programs and scholarship.
Increase education retention and participation.

The culminating activity for the MOVE program was for the students to attend and receive VIP status at the Latin Sound '99 event at the Hollywood Bowl. The students heard music played by the Buena Vista Social Club, Hothouse, the LSI Student Salsa All-Stars, and the CalArts Latin Orchestra directed by David Roitstein.

Cribs in the Classroom

In teacher Janet Grane's classroom, teen parents, girls, and boys attended class with nonparenting teens on a full-time basis rather than being placed in an independent studies program. Students without babies learned the nonromantic responsibility and real-life impact of raising an infant. The teen parents received support from

Reflective Practices:
Perspectives of Multi-Unicultural School
Leaders

classmates, a public health nurse, and social service workers. The classroom was equipped with standard classroom equipment, but also had several bay cribs, swings, and changing tables. Students learned how to make patchwork quilts for the cribs made on sewing machines that were purchased through California lottery funds.

Campus Canine

Through the continued processes of reflection by the Chaffey West principal and staff, the chance to provide learning opportunities for students are seized when situations arise. That moment happened when a stray dog entered the classroom of teacher Janet Grane after lying in front of the opened classroom door for several days. Several "hard-core" students who had known ties to several local gangs welcomed the dog into the classroom and named the dog Rosie. Rosie the canine served in the capacity of a classroom mascot and therapy dog in the classroom. Rosie had made such an impact on the learning dynamics in the classroom that an article was published in the May 1997 issue of Dog Fancy Magazine. In the "Dogs That Make a Difference" section of the magazine, award-winning writer and author Betsy Sikora Siino (1997) stated,

In no time, Rosie blossomed into her role as a self-taught therapy dog, soothing students with her presence and acting as an educational inspiration. As a living, breathing example, Rosie sparked interest in learning among students. They learned about canine and human physiology by constructing "visible dog" models, marveled at the similarities in behavior in wolf and human "packs" and compared canine and human senses. (p. 25)

The teacher Janet Grane developed lessons in the core subject areas to provide learning experiences that were part of subject-based standards. The teacher listed some "canine curriculum concepts" learning activities that related to subject areas.

Canine Curriculum Concepts

Language Arts

Call of the Wild, J. London
Travels with Charlie, J. Steinbeck
Many other short stories, novels, essays, points of view, and report writing

Social Studies

Areas and purpose of various breed origins, government regulations, laws governing dog ownership, history, and time of breed origins

Science
Use of visible dog models, five senses, internal organs, growth, behavioral

Dr. Paul A. Rodríguez & Dr. Roberto F. Casas

experiments, genetics, diseases, and vaccines

Math
Learn the seven of multiplication tables, budgeting, food and accessory comparison-shopping

Humanities
Learn about euthanasia and vivisection

Tolerance
Different colors of dogs, sizes (all breeds)

Vocational
Learn about various careers such as groomer, veterinary assistant, dog sitter, and lab technician

Ghetto Garden

In the parking lot of Chaffey West, there was a section of dirt that sat barren with weeds growing from the earth. Once again, through the process of reflection, the principal supported the concept of planting a garden for students to maintain.

Approximately one hundred square feet of a plot of dirt was converted into a garden at this inner-city school. Students developed a taste of faith when seeds sprouted, and plants produced vegetables through the nurturing of students. The cucumbers were turned into pickles, and pumpkins were harvested and decorated then made into pies. The simple addition of a half-dozen flowering plants that were culled from the teacher's yard resulted in the landlord installing attractive landscaping and repairing the automatic sprinkler system after five years of disrepair.

Reflection to Empowerment

Through the process of reflection of instructional learning practices, the principal provided the environment for shared decision making and for the support of

Dr. Paul A. Rodríguez & Dr. Roberto F. Casas

teachers to develop learning experiences for students that were unorthodox in nature, and that required students to think and participate in ways that were foreign to them. Through the leadership of the principal and the creativity of the teachers, students participated in learning activities that enhanced their abilities for lifelong learning and to acquire basic skills to be competitive. If education is valued after high school, then it should be valued during high school. Teachers are privileged and strapped with the responsibility of helping students become intrinsic and overt learners who will make connections with society and the global marketplace. Teachers must be empowered to teach out of the traditional manner in spite of standards and prepare students for the new era. Teachers, more than administrators, must take on leadership roles that go beyond teaching subject matter. This process can only happen if there are principals and school leaders who embrace

Reflective Practices:
Perspectives of Multi-Unicultural School Leaders

reflective practice. As reiterated by Osterman and Kottkamp (1993),

Reflective practice is one of the most significant new developments to influence the educational community, but until now, there has been no practical guide to its implementation. At last, everyone who has an interest in the improvement of education can explore a leading-edge strategy that empowers and motivates people through ongoing process of professional development. Reflective practice for educators clearly demonstrates that theory and practice are inseparable: to change the way we do things, we must first understand what we do now and why we do it before we can adopt new methods. (p. 205)

In May of 1999, while writer Roberto Casas was working on his doctorate, he was able to take a survey that gave him feedback or a personal evaluation of his thinking

Dr. Paul A. Rodríguez & Dr. Roberto F. Casas

through the completion of "Brain Works" as part of a course entitled Educational Leadership Appraisal (Ellis 2000). Casas (2000) stated that he was able to better understand how and why he made decisions as a school leader. Based on the results of the personal evaluation, Casas was given the following feedback:

Roberto, you are mildly left-hemisphere dominant while showing a slight preference for auditory processing. This overall combination seems to indicate a well-working blend of logic and judgment and organization, with sufficient intuition, perception and creativity to balance the dominance.

You will at times experience conflict between how you feel and what you think which will generally be resolved in favor of what you think. You will find yourself interested in the practical applications of whatever material you have learned or whatever knowledge you posses or aspects

Reflective Practices:
Perspectives of Multi-Unicultural School
Leaders

of whatever position you are in. Largely, you will orient yourself toward intellectual activities and structure. Though not rigid, you will schedule yourself, plan, and focus on routine and continuity of operations, rather than on changes and disruptions. When changes or disruptions occur, you are likely to consider first how to ensure that such disruptions do not occur again in the given future.

The same balance is reflected in your sensory preference. You will tend to be reflective and measured in your interaction style. For the most part, you will be considered objective without being cold and goal-oriented while retaining the capacity to listen to others. Preferentially you learn by listening and maintaining significant internal dialogues with yourself. Nevertheless, you have sufficient visualization capabilities to benefit from using graphs, charts, doodles, or even body movement to enhance your comprehension and memory.

Dr. Paul A. Rodríguez & Dr. Roberto F. Casas

To the extent that you are even implicitly aware of your hemispheric dominance and sensory style, you will feel most comfortable in those arenas, which emphasize verbal skills and logic. Teaching, law and science are those that stand out among the professions, along with technical sales and management.

Strategies and Considerations

One might ask, "Why do followers subordinate themselves not to an individual who is utterly different but to a member of their group who has authority at this time and who is fundamentally the same as they are and who at times is prepared to be a follower just as they are?" The leader inevitably embodies many qualities of the followers. Reflective leaders develop the capacity of their subordinates to take leadership roles and actions.

CHAPTER 4
Guidelines for Engaging in Reflective Practice

Reflective practice can be a rather important tool in professional development and in practice-based professional learning situations. Individuals learning from their own professional and personal experiences, rather than from pedagogy or knowledge transfer, may well be the personal source of professional development for both school principals and teachers. As such, the notion of reflective practice, especially in professional development has been widely used for practitioners in areas such as education and healthcare. However, the question is, Does learning from experiences have a wider relevance to organizational learning environments? Why? Reflective practice (Leitch, Day 2000) argues, "The appeal of the use of reflective practice for teachers is that as teaching and learning are complex, and there is not one right approach,

Dr. Paul A. Rodríguez & Dr. Roberto F. Casas

reflecting on different versions of teaching and reshaping past and current experiences will lead to improvement in teaching practices." Further, Leitch and Day (2000) state, "In implementing a process of Reflective Practice teachers will be able to move themselves, and their schools, beyond existing theories in practice."

Reflective practice is associated with learning from experience and can be viewed as an important strategy for school leaders who embrace change for school improvement and student achievement. Due to the complex and continually changing educational environment, principals and school site leaders could benefit from suggested ways for them to practice reflective leadership. Listed below are suggested simple guidelines for daily reflective practice for school leaders:

Keep a journal of activities; note your actions.

Reflective Practices:
Perspectives of Multi-Unicultural School Leaders

Seek feedback from school stakeholders of your decisions/actions.
View experiences objectively.
Take time at the end of each day, meeting, experience, etc., to reflect on actions.

According to Osterman and Kottkamp (1993),

Reflective practice is a human resource strategy. Sorely missing from discussions of school reform, this theoretical perspective maintains that organizations and people depend on one another and that processes that satisfy human needs also serve organizational needs. Reflective practice is a process that empowers and motivates individuals and groups through ongoing process of professional development. In this process, as people begin to envision new possibilities and to work together in different ways to achieve newly defined goals, the possibilities of change on a broader level becomes more real. (p. 186)

Strategies and Considerations

The concept of reflective practice hinges on the idea of lifelong learning where practitioners analyze their experiences in order to learn from them. Reflective practice is used to promote independent professionals who are continuously engaged in the reflection of situations they encounter in their professional worlds.

CHAPTER 5
QUALITIES OF EFFECTIVE LEADERSHIP: PRINCIPLES OF PETER F. DRUCKER

Knowledge has to be improved, challenged, and increased constantly or it vanishes.

—Peter F. Drucker

Introduction

As we approach the third millennium, America cries out for leadership at all levels of society and in every organization that composes it. It must be a national priority to seek out effective leaders. We urgently need culturally sensitive women and men who can grasp the vision of the future. Leadership is the essential force behind any successful organization. Effective leaders help generate vital and viable organizations that can develop and mobilize into new visionary roles in today's modern society. In so doing, leaders can form a more desirable future for this nation and the world. In contrast, ineffective leadership directs society into becoming a dreamless society, lacking purpose, vision, and cohesion. Bennis states the following:

Leaders are the ones with vision, who inspire others and cause them to galvanize their efforts and achieve change. Managers, on the other hand, will follow standard operating procedure to their graves, if necessary, because they do not possess the ability to change course. (Bennis 1997, 17)

Leadership Paradigm: Traits, Behaviors, and Qualities

The study of leadership has focused on traits, behavior, and more recently, qualities that create leadership.
The trait views of leadership focus on having the right stuff and are concerned with which leaders are.

Reflective Practices:
Perspectives of Multi-Unicultural School
Leaders

Another perspective examines leader behavior, for as Greenberg and Baron (2000) note, we "may not be born with the 'right stuff,' but we certainly strive to do the 'right things'—that is, to do what it takes to become a leader."

Studies have looked more holistically between leaders and followers.

Creating Tomorrow's Society of Citizens

Leaders have a commitment to self-assessment as a commitment to developing themselves and their organization as a leader.

Leaders have a commitment to community and to change lives.

Self-assessment is the first action requirement of leadership that is constantly reshaping.

We are creating tomorrow's society of citizens through the social sector everybody is a leader, everybody is responsible,

everybody. Self-assessment can and should convert good intentions and knowledge into effective action—not next year, but tomorrow morning.
—Peter F. Drucker

Leadership Traits

The trait view of leadership suggests that individuals become leaders because of the traits they possess.
In short, people become leaders because in some special way they are different from others.
Green (2001) notes, "Such traits or characteristics can be classified under the headings of capacity, friendliness, achievement, responsibility, participation and status."
House, Shane, and Herold (1996) have found that successful leaders possess many of the following traits: drive, honesty and integrity, leadership motivation, self-confidence, cognitive ability, creativity, and flexibility.

Reflective Practices:
Perspectives of Multi-Unicultural School
Leaders

Individuals who posses these traits are thought to be good leaders.

Leaders are not like other people . . . they do not need to have the 'right stuff' and this stuff is not equally present in all people. Leadership is a demanding, unrelenting job . . . and it would be a profound disservice to leaders to suggest that they are ordinary people . . . in the realm of leadership . . . the individual does matter. (Kirkpatrick and Locke 1991)

Trait theory suggests that the more traits a leader possess the more effective the leader. Trait theory also matches the hierarchical organizational structure, and successful leaders, those with the key traits, are placed in top positions within the organization.

What is our mission?

Dr. Paul A. Rodríguez & Dr. Roberto F. Casas

The core mission remains fixed while operating practices, cultural norms, strategies, tactics, processes, structures, and methods continually change in response to changing realities.
The core mission provides guidance, not just about what to do, but equally what not to do.
People will demand operating autonomy—freedom plus responsibility—and will simultaneously demand that the organizations of which they are a part stand for something.

Leadership Behaviors

Autocratic/authoritarian behaviors tend to be controlling with the sole responsibility for decision-making and action resting with the leader.
Such people tend to be directive and controlling in their actions toward others, and leaders with behaviors that cluster at this end of the continuum tend to run the show, tell people when and where to do

Reflective Practices:
Perspectives of Multi-Unicultural School
Leaders

things, and do not like their authority or decisions and actions questioned.

Leaders in the democratic/participative end of the continuum tend to share in decision-making and courses of action.

They encourage others to participate in the what, when, and how questions they confront daily and are therefore seen as collegial and collaborative in their behavior.

Autocratic/Authoritarian Behaviors	Democratic/Participative Behaviors
Controlling Directive Sole decision maker Total responsibility of action Does not delegate Closed to others' input Makes quick decisions and abandons input from others— egocentric	Delegator Cooperative Collegial Shares in decision making Open to suggestions Shares responsibility for action Open communication Active listener

Dr. Paul A. Rodríguez & Dr. Roberto F. Casas

Leadership Behaviors

Supportive leadership: seeks to maintain a supportive relationship in the workplace and demonstrates consideration and awareness of the needs of others.
Directive leadership: sets standards for success, communicates performance standards, schedules the work, and provides specific directions for accomplishing the task.
Participative leadership: involves consulting with others and seeking opinions of others concerning task completion or other work-related activities.
Achievement-oriented leadership: emphasizes excellence in task completion and sets goals that are challenging yet attainable.

Many organizations focus toward self-managed teams.

Reflective Practices:
Perspectives of Multi-Unicultural School
Leaders

Guidelines to help leaders build self-managed teams	Overall leadership qualities and the interactive nature of leadership
Build trust, inspire teamwork, and empower others Clarify team purpose and values Expand team capability by recognizing and affirming optimal performance Create team identity through relationships building and communication Be flexible and make the most of team differences Practice active listening with all team members Practice open communication Have faith in yourself; know yourself	The ability to create and use culture that guides all members of the organization The ability to use interpersonal skills in building trust and working with others The ability to model personal integrity and responsibility in interacting with others The ability to diagnose problems, select protocols and procedures based on equity, and take risks The ability to unite effort with purpose to obtain results

These qualities have the appearance of being related to traits or behaviors, but the key difference is the interpersonal application as leaders interact with various constituencies of the organization. The nature of this interaction between leaders and others can be characterized as charismatic or transformational leadership.

Charismatic Leaders

Charismatic leaders have that something special about them and exert especially powerful effects on followers.
A special kind of leader-follower relationship develops those results in higher level of enthusiasm and excitement. The charismatic leaders can make ordinary people do extraordinary things.

Transformational Leaders
Transformational leaders also have charisma but are able to incorporate the leader qualities in such a way that they are

Reflective Practices:
Perspectives of Multi-Unicultural School Leaders

able to transform and renew their organizations.

Transformational leaders not only inspire, but also captivate strong emotions to teach and change followers.

Transformational leaders tap into cognitive processes by helping others to be problem solvers while providing support to individuals by giving them attention and encouragement.

Transformational leadership focuses on the leader's ability to provide shared values and a vision for the future.

Hoy and Miskel (1996) view transformational leaders that exhibit the following:

Define the need for change
Create new visions and muster commitment to the visions
Concentrate on long-term goals
Inspire followers to transcend their own interests for higher order goals

Dr. Paul A. Rodríguez & Dr. Roberto F. Casas

Change the organization to accommodate a new vision, rather than work within the existing one
Mentor followers to take greater responsibility for their own development and that of others. Followers become leaders and leaders become change agents and ultimately transform the organization (p. 393)

Transformational leaders are able to manage the boundaries of autocratic and democratic decision making, making them values-led, people-centered, achievement-oriented, and able to manage a number of ongoing tensions and dilemmas. Transformational leaders must provide intellectual stimulation, individualized consideration, and inspirational motivation as they work within their organization.

Leaders must know who their customers are and what their customers value. As Drucker points out, in any organization, the customer is one step

Reflective Practices:
Perspectives of Multi-Unicultural School Leaders

ahead of you.
Leaders and organizations that are devoted to results—will always regard this to its basic integrity—will adapt and change as they do. As Peter Drucker puts it, "Your success ultimately depends on what you have contributed to the success of your customers."

Understand Your Assumptions	What Does the Primary Customer Value	What Do Supporting Customers Value	Listen to Your Customers
*Make assumptions based on customer interpretations *Begin with assumptions and find out what you believe your customers are saying *Find the difference *Assess your results	*Make a commitment to what the customer values most *Work on the problems of the primary customer *Primary customers' relationship is greater, as are the organizations' results	What the primary customers value is of utmost importance *Understand equally what supporting customers value *Knowing all your customers' values is essential and each defines values differently	*Listen and understand each of your constituencies' concerns *Listen to customers and accept what they value as objective fact *Make sure your customer's voice is part of your discussions and decisions

Dr. Paul A. Rodríguez & Dr. Roberto F. Casas

Transformational leaders are at the heart of the organization. They are change agents who look beyond immediate needs of the organization and focus on long-term goals.

What are our results?

Peter Drucker emphasizes the following:

Leadership is Accountable	Mission Must Yield Reasonable Results
*Leaders need a systematic analysis as part of their plans * Leaders determine what results for the organization should be and where to concentrate for future success *The mission defines the scope of the leader's responsibility *Leadership is accountable to determine what must be appraised and judged to protect the organization from failure and ensure meaningful results	*Results and plan must produce some measurable outcomes *Results and plan must build mechanisms that allow midcourse corrections based on these results *Goal is to achieve real impact *Hard work is indispensable to success *Ultimately, what is at the very heart of the plan and results is how the lives of people are improved

Reflective Practices:
Perspectives of Multi-Unicultural School
Leaders

What is our plan?

Drucker understood that goals flow from mission, aim the organization where it must go, build on strength, address opportunity, and taken all together, outline your desired future.
The Drucker Foundation's vision is stated as follows:

A society that recognizes the social sector as the leading force in creating healthy communities and improving the quality of life, building around mission and long-term goals is the only way to integrate short-term interests. Your plan leads you to results.

Five Elements of Effective Plan

Abandonment—deciding whether to abandon what does not work, what has never worked
Concentration—building on success, strengthening what does work

Dr. Paul A. Rodríguez & Dr. Roberto F. Casas

Innovation—look for tomorrow's success, the true innovations, and the diversity that stirs the imagination
Risk taking—you must balance the short range with the long. There is no formula for risk-taking decisions.
Analysis—recognize when you do not know; when you are not yet sure whether to abandon, concentrate, go into something new, or take a particular risk

Continuously revisit your action steps

Action steps establish accountability for objectives. Leadership requires constant sharpening, refocusing, never really being satisfied.

Cycle of Organizational Renewal and Becoming

Transformational leaders must pass through eight milestones that are relevant and viable for effective organizations. These milestones are important for small

***Reflective Practices:
Perspectives of Multi-Unicultural School
Leaders***

organizations, large businesses, educational institutions, and government agencies

Elements of Eight Milestones

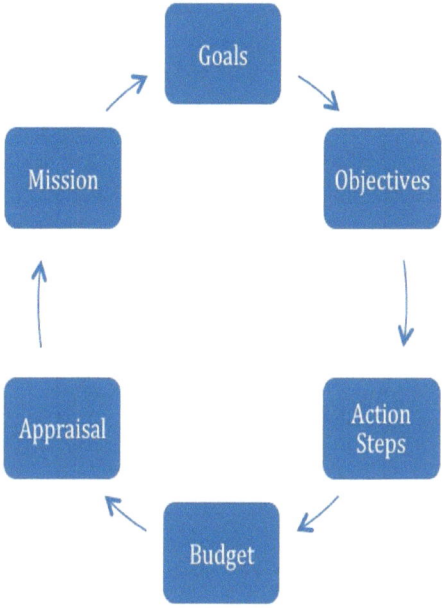

Dr. Paul A. Rodríguez & Dr. Roberto F. Casas

- Scan the environment
- Revisit the Mission
- Run the hierarchy
- Challenge the gospel
- Employ the power of language
- Disperse leadership across the organization
- Lead from the front, don't push from the rear
- Assess performance

Scan the environment—means to understand the assessment of emerging trends—not after. These trends provide essential background for planning change. Revisit the mission—means to revisit the mission and the first questions of the five most important questions that Peter

Drucker points out:

What is our mission?

*Reflective Practices:
Perspectives of Multi-Unicultural School
Leaders*

Who is our customer?
What does the customer value?
Ban the hierarchy—transformation requires moving people out of their organizational boxes into flexible, fluid management systems. Job rotation becomes an enriching reality.
Challenge the gospel—means to build to meet the future. There should be no sacred cows, as everyone should be challenged.
Employ the power of language—leaders need to be clear and consistent in their messages to their customers, constituents and repeat their messages repeatedly.
Disperse leadership across the organization—leadership is a responsibility shared by all members of the organization.
Lead from the front; don't push from the rear—means leaders model desired behaviors, never break a promise, and know that leadership is a matter of how to be, not how to do it.
Assess performance—means self-assessment is essential to progress. Ask

yourself Peter Ducker's last two questions: What are our results? Moreover, What is our plan?

Peter Drucker advises us that though we may know the milestones on our journey, the future remains unexplored. Every leader and organization needs to focus on the quality of their mission and the leadership it inspires for future success.

Conclusions
There are some key assumptions that drive the capacity for building leadership in organizations. These assumptions include the following:

Leadership and leader are not the same, and leadership is not based on traits. Leadership is a reciprocal learning process that allows individuals to construct and validate meanings that result in shared goals and purposes.

Reflective Practices:
Perspectives of Multi-Unicultural School
Leaders

Leadership is a process that everyone in the organization can engage in and involves skilled and complicated work. Leadership involves sharing decision making with others and is a collective endeavor, and the journey of learning leadership must be appreciated in order for the purpose and action to be shared. Leadership is collaborative in nature and involves the sharing of power and authority in order to empower others.

Leadership Principles to Follow for Success in the Twenty-First Century

Leadership is a sacred trust, not bestowed rights and involves knowing your core values. Ethical behavior and your integrity are essential at all times, for others will test you often.

Leadership is about hearing all the voices—customers, workers, community, and others. Active listening and open communication is necessary.

Dr. Paul A. Rodríguez & Dr. Roberto F. Casas

Leadership is about creating an excess of vision—yours, mine, and ours.
Leadership is about being uncomfortable, looking for data that disconfirms what we believe to be true.
Leadership is about a journey that begins with introspection and reflection, self-assessment, and keeping your vision focused and consistent
Leadership is about empowering yourselves and others, sharing information and decision-making, taking risks that will continue the vision and mission of the organization.
Leadership involves identifying and dealing with personal behaviors to change, both personal and organizational.
Trust is the foundation on which success is built, as well as conviction to keep focused on your goals, values, integrity, commitment, and vision.
Building positive working relationships where the leaders makes their intentions known to others and solicit feedback. Building on active listening and open

communication with all individuals, they encounter.

Such feedback helps all involved parties to be more consistent, behave in trusting, and compassionate ways.

The sharing of values and hopes helps to establish an organizational vision and culture.

Executive Skills Inherent to Leadership

Definitions

Executive Skills

Definitions:
Executive skills are developed slowly over time through childhood and adolescence and are not usually fully developed until the mid-twenties. They are required to successfully complete tasks (take an idea from start to finish).

Dr. Paul A. Rodríguez & Dr. Roberto F. Casas

Response inhibition: the ability to think before acting and to resist the urge to say something
Working memory: the ability to hold information in memory while performing a task with that information (math, word problems)
Emotional control: the ability to manage emotions to achieve goals, complete tasks, or control and direct behavior
Sustained attention: the capacity to maintain attention to a situation or task in spite of distractions, fatigue, or boredom
Task initiation: the ability to begin a task without undue procrastination in a timely manner
Planning/prioritization: the ability to figure out how to reach a goal or complete a task
Organization: the ability to create and maintain systems to keep track of information or materials
Time management: the ability to gauge how much time one has, how to allocate it, and stay within time limits and deadlines

Reflective Practices:
Perspectives of Multi-Unicultural School Leaders

Goal-directed persistence: the capacity to have a goal and follow through to completion despite distractions of competing interests

Flexibility: the ability to revise plans in the face of obstacles, setbacks, new information, or mistakes

Resilience

Definition:
It is the ability to bounce back from setbacks, learn from failures, be motivated by challenges, and believe you can handle stress and difficulties in life. It is not all or nothing. It comes in amounts. You can be a little resilient, a lot resilient, or resilient in some situations but not others.

Six Ingredients of Resilience We Need to Embrace in Our Leadership Roles

Dr. Paul A. Rodríguez & Dr. Roberto F. Casas

It means being comfortable with feelings and being able to express them. Resilient leaders do not get "stuck" in an emotion. Resilience does not stop you from having impulses that are not in your best interest, but you can learn to internalize the "stop-and-think" message, and use it to make appropriate choices about your actions and decisions.
Optimistic people are happier, healthier, and more productive, have better relationships, succeed more, are better problem solvers, and are less likely to become depressed.
It increases the likelihood that you will be able to come up with solutions to a problem you are facing (Plan B).

Self-confidence: you know your strengths, and use them to navigate your world (sense of humor, charm, and creativity).
It facilitates strong relationships. When leaders have a strong network of friends and colleagues who care about them (support system), they have someone to

whom they can turn to when they need help.

Strategies and Considerations

Every individual has the capacity for leadership. It begins with self-assessment and understanding their strengths and opportunities for improvement. Every individual needs to consider the relationships established, not for their personal gains, but for the good of society as a whole. Leadership is not a position, but a collection of responsibilities that follow strategic paths.

What is your mission?
Who are your customers?
What do your customers value?
What are your results?
What is your plan?

Dr. Paul A. Rodríguez & Dr. Roberto F. Casas

CHAPTER 6
REFLECTION ON A LEADERSHIP-VALUE SYSTEM

Leaders typically have the power to choose a decision-making process to solve conflict. Clearly, leaders must measure the level of importance of conflict and the type of process to be used (consultative, participative, autocratic, or consensual). The key to decision making is being able to adapt to situations. Adaptation to situational events may typically derive from experiences.

Often times, we make decisions based on our value system and through our knowledge of outcomes from experiences. Leaders may reflect on experiences and struggle with internal contradictions in values, beliefs, and habits. Heifetz (1994) asserts, "Leadership arouses passion. The exercise and even the study of leadership stir feeling because leadership engages our values. Indeed the term itself is value-

Reflective Practices:
Perspectives of Multi-Unicultural School Leaders

laden." Heifetz states that "the term leadership involves our self-images and moral codes" (p. 13). Individual school leaders form beliefs and a core set of values. In Deal and Peterson (1999) they state that Principal Sigmund Boloz wrote the following poem that depicts his core obligations:

The C Diet

My job is;

To keep the compass
To massage change
To build credibility: a positive image for the school in the eyes of the community
To cultivate my staff
To ask compelling questions
To be an advocate for children
I build the culture of the school
Curriculum, consensus, constituents, community

Dr. Paul A. Rodríguez & Dr. Roberto F. Casas

I see my job as building my staff. I strive to build:

Confidence in themselves, in their decisions and in their teaching
Courage to take risks and to break new ground
Compassion for children and others
Character to always do their personal best
Competence that they know the current trends
Capacity to learn new things
Commitment to our mission
Clarity a good focus on the what's and the how's
Consciousness to bring thinking to a higher level
Communication open lines of dialect
Collaboration share expertise
Collegiality professional interactions
Challenge to keep staff on their cutting edge
Critical thinking thoughtfulness
Creativity to implement innovation
Curiosity actively seek better ways

Reflective Practices:
Perspectives of Multi-Unicultural School Leaders

Contentment feel accepted (p. 18)
Copyright: Sigmund Boloz, 1997, reprinted by permission

Ott (1989) provides a simple definition of values and beliefs. Ott states, "Values are the conscious expressions of what an organization stands for. Values define a standard of goodness, quality, or excellence that undergirds behavior and decision making, and what people care about. Beliefs are how we comprehend and deal with the world around us. They are consciously held, cognitive views about truth and reality" (Ott 1989, p. 39). Deal and Peterson (1999) expound, "Beliefs originate in group and personal experiences and through reading books and articles. Beliefs are powerful in schools because they represent the core understandings about student capacity (immutable or alterable), teacher responsibility for learning (little or a lot), expert sources of teacher knowledge (experience, research, or intention), and educational success (will never happen or is achievable)" (p. 27).

"Minority school leaders bring 'to the table' everyday through their actions; values, beliefs and reflective practice. These actions are often viewed as assumptions and norms and serve as 'behavioral blueprints' that people are supposed to follow; they are organizational sea anchors providing predictability and stability" (Ott 1989, p. 37). Minority school leaders bring experience, knowledge, expertise, cultural, ethnic values and assumptions to their actions. Deal and Peterson (1999) declare, "Cultural assumptions are hard to assess because they are so closely aligned with myths." However, it has been my experience that "cultural assumptions" are derived by core beliefs and "gut feelings," which are also difficult to assess.

School Culture and Values: Internal and External

Reflective Practices:
Perspectives of Multi-Unicultural School Leaders

Too often, school culture can become exclusionary, distant, and out of touch with community morals and values. In some schools, the culture and climate encourages staff to come together, exclude, and shut out parents. This strategy has served as the norm in some schools with high enrollments of minority and foreign-born students. Often times, parents speak different languages, have various interaction styles and educational beliefs and levels that too often cause a divide between professionals working inside the schools and parents waiting outside the schools. Leading and building a cohesive school community means designing a culture and climate that "extends a hand" and touches all stakeholders of the school community (students, teachers, staff, administrators, parents/guardians, and the school's neighborhood). Reflective leaders know by intuition that building a positive and inclusive school culture and climate will ensure student academic success. A

Dr. Paul A. Rodríguez & Dr. Roberto F. Casas

community center where parents and neighborhood volunteers can participate and serve further ensures student success.

Reflective school leaders know through data and best practices that student support programs, such as Response to Intervention II (RtI-2), will help all students that are not at or at below grade level. This strategy, by virtue of a school's "pyramid of interventions," will help the school community to become school academic partners.

According to Deal and Peterson (1999),

Leaders need the skills and knowledge to uncover a culture's deeper history. They need the techniques to assess current conditions and values. Moreover, most important, they require the ability to be symbolic leaders and cultural reinforces in their daily work. For some, these skills can be developed on the job; others will go through preparation programs.

Reflective Practices:
Perspectives of Multi-Unicultural School Leaders

Nevertheless, many will need in-depth professional development opportunities with adequate time to reflect, analyze, and interpret their culture. (p. 142)

Strategies and Considerations

In retrospect, leaders who reflect and develop sound practices through experience and introspection will be empowered at both the individual and the organizational levels; reflection is a powerful multilevel source for individual and systematic change.

CHAPTER 7
Leaders Must Adapt through Change with Restraint

Reflective practice is a potentially powerful avenue for school
improvement and systemic change.

Osterman and Kottkamp (1993) exclaim, "To try reflective practice seriously means calling off 'business as usual' and trusting professional educators and parents in ways not even considered under many contemporary reform proposals and our pervasive way of doing things" (p. 188). They continue:

To try it seriously means accepting on a broad front the kinds of beliefs and attitudes we recommended for facilitators. To try it seriously means those in traditional power positions in schools, districts state departments of education, governor's offices, and legislatures will need to trust those in the field to improve education and

Reflective Practices:
Perspectives of Multi-Unicultural School
Leaders

give them adequate time to develop, implement, assess and revise action alternatives. To try it seriously means academics in professional preparation programs need to relinquish control over the learning process by becoming less didactic, information oriented, and more focused on the link between the classroom and the world of practice. (p. 188)

Cultural Proficiency through Reflection

Coauthors Franco, Ott, and Robles (2011) describe how they, as Latinas, all became school superintendents; they share stories of their childhoods, their careers, their educational and life challenges, their vision and core beliefs on how to transform schools into environments of equity and excellence. What these three Latinas have in common is their life experiences and cultural similarities providing the process of reflection and reflective practice. They stated that they are baby boomers that

Dr. Paul A. Rodríguez & Dr. Roberto F. Casas

were raised during the Vietnam era and through the major societal changes such as integration, the demographic shifts of the population in the United States of America, and the nation's quest to place emphasis on accountability and how to tackle the achievement gaps. The three wrote a book together based on their experiences titled Leadership for Equity: A Culturally Proficient Begins in School (2011).

Franco (2011) reflects on how her early upbringing in a large extended family and living in a culturally diverse neighborhood—where Spanish, Italian, and English were the daily languages—helped to develop her cultural proficiency. She explains how she had to adapt when her family had to move to Los Angeles from Pueblo, Colorado, for economic reasons (p. 13).

Ott (2011) recalls her initial upbringing in Germany, where she was born Maria Miranda Gutierrez. She was born to a father serving in the US military, whose

Reflective Practices:
Perspectives of Multi-Unicultural School Leaders

family emigrated from Mexico to California, and her German mother was from Bavaria, Germany. She stated that at five years of age, she moved from Germany to East Los Angeles, California. She remembers her struggles as an English language learner, which helped her reflect on her quest to become a lifelong advocate for children learning English as a second language (p. 13).

Further, Robles (2011) describes starting kindergarten at the age of four and having to move several times during her early childhood. Robles stated, "The moves helped me adapt and be flexible in new environments" (p. 13). She reflects and remembers that being raised in diverse settings helped her appreciate many cultures, but it was where she also observed biases and insensitivities (p. 13). The coauthors state, "We developed an understanding and appreciation of our shared experiences and those unique to each one of us. We found that many painful situations that reflected our culture, language or female identity were hidden under the exterior of our professional successes"(p. 13).

Reflection for a Sense of Purpose

Reflective practice is not a passing phase or one of the many fads that have inflicted public education over the years. Reflection itself forces us as educational leaders to look intrinsically at our core. It forces us to continue questioning our leadership and the impact; it is going to have on our children and families that we serve. Reflection drives the perceptions of others regarding our leadership. It is our belief that in order to close the achievement gap of our students, each one of us has to reflect on what we bring to the table. Once we reflect on and determine our strengths and areas for improvement, then and only then, can we begin to provide the process of closing the gap of achievement for our students?

Reflective Practices:
Perspectives of Multi-Unicultural School
Leaders
Strategies and Considerations

The reflections of these three Latina superintendents give us another example of leadership through self-reflection and professional and cultural experiences. The readers may develop ways of including their own reflective practices through their own introspections.

Dr. Paul A. Rodríguez & Dr. Roberto F. Casas

CHAPTER 8
Vail High School: A Mosaic of Backgrounds for Change

Vail High School is the continuation high school in the Montebello Unified School District. With a student population of over four hundred students, Vail reflects a mosaic of backgrounds with different needs and characteristics. In the sixty-five-year history of Vail High School, there has never been a Hispanic principal. The students form a unique montage of diversity including, but not limited to, socioeconomic status, linguistic ability, personal mannerisms, motivational attitudes, social and academic abilities. The road to adult destinations would necessitate different routes with a blend of instructional methods. Vail High School provided excellent opportunities to enhance student success.

The WASC (Western Association for Schools and Colleges) and CDE (California

Reflective Practices:
Perspectives of Multi-Unicultural School
Leaders

Department of Education) joint process for Focus on Learning served as an excellent guideline to assist with the determination of student progress and success. The focused attention for change was directed to the schoolwide critical areas within the schoolwide action plan. Intense involvement evolved from individual groups who were most affected by the schoolwide action plan and schoolwide areas that included the students, staff, administration, and school community.

Vail High School Developments: 2007–2010

Vail High School budget reductions during 2007 to 2008 included a reduction of the full-time literacy coach, two FTEs (full-time employees, certificated), one FTE guidance counselor, one hour for instructional media assistant, LEP (Limited English Program), and assistant principal position was eliminated and replaced with a dean of

Dr. Paul A. Rodríguez & Dr. Roberto F. Casas

students position. With the loss of the literacy coach, the focus for student achievement was redirected from both reading and writing to only writing. The loss of one guidance counselor and assistant principal position influenced student services. To date, there remains only one guidance counselor for student services.
Overview

Vail High School was due for change. The new principal, staff, supporting staff, and school community were challenged to make the changes that were conducive for student academic, personal, social, and career achievements. With the leadership of the principal, staff members volunteered to serve as focus group leaders and become members of the leadership team. Leadership team met Thursday afternoons during the school year to further develop and delineate goals and objectives of the schoolwide action plan. Groups were formed to address and complete the following tasks:

Reflective Practices:
Perspectives of Multi-Unicultural School
Leaders

Outline areas of the plan that had been met that were works in progress, or had not been addressed
Develop a timeline that was more fluid and specific to curricular changes occurring at the site and district levels
Assign groups of teachers to address each third-year progress report

Organization: Vision and Purpose, Governance, Leadership, Staff, and Resources

The leadership team collected and shared data with the site administrator and entire teaching staff. The language arts, science, and math departments recommended to school site administration to allocate one Monday per month for staff department meetings. These collaborative meetings focused on utilizing data to enhance the quality of educational decisions as well as strong, stellar instructional practices.

Dr. Paul A. Rodríguez & Dr. Roberto F. Casas

The inclusion of a parent-involvement program included a new TeleParent system as well as personal, direct parent calls that took place to enhance the parent-involvement component at Vail High School. The administration also maintained contact with parents through one-to-one meetings and group gatherings. Teachers welcomed parent visitations before and after the school day. Teachers' phone extensions were given to parents upon request to encourage and monitor student attendance, academic growth, and progress. In addition, Vail High School's updated school website offered parents and the community current schedules and upcoming events. The website also provided parents and community access to Vail High School's Facebook and Twitter web pages for additional information.

College entrance requirements were enhanced with after-school adult education

Reflective Practices:
Perspectives of Multi-Unicultural School Leaders

credit-recovery labs that are available to the students served at Vail High School.
Vail High School offered classes from East Los Angeles College, where students were concurrently enrolled, Regional Opportunity Program classes (ROP), and after-school courses through a district-funded after-school federal grant. The students at Vail High School were thoroughly immerged in A-G CSU/UC requirements. As part of the monitoring component, all student transcripts were made available upon request to determine student progress. The staff and administration of Vail High School set-aside opportunities for the students to understand how to interpret their own transcripts. Students have been enabled to understand and embrace their own academic progress through this new opportunity. The leadership team worked together with the entire faculty and administration to ensure clear guidelines for staff development. In addition, committees

meeting were implemented, monitored, and maintained on a daily and weekly basis.

Standards-Based Learning: Curriculum

Language arts teacher has integrated standards-based concepts across the curriculum. The social-science department integrated math and language-arts concepts in their history, language, and health classes. Reading in the content areas was approached. Syllabus standardization across all disciplines/departments has been implemented at Vail High School. TeleParent is utilized schoolwide to inform parents of their children's academic progress. Teacher and parent one-on-one conferences are greatly encouraged by administration. Administration has an open-door policy with all staff, parents, students and community members. Data from the analysis of student performance has encouraged the coordination of lessons. The math department implemented the

Reflective Practices:
Perspectives of Multi-Unicultural School
Leaders

newly updated Algebra I curriculum with coordinating units, challenge tests, and benchmark assessments. Edu-Soft and EZ Grade Pro are utilized for the evaluative component. The Vail High School staff encourages an 80 percent classroom attendance rate for each subject. Students became more responsible for their classroom instruction and work. Implementation of the 80 percent of classroom attendance has enabled Vail High School's overall school attendance rate to escalate from 70 percent to 90.29 percent in two years.

Teachers utilized individual learning plans (ILP). Teachers share data to understand the student's strengths and areas of need for opportunities for growth. When students initially enroll into Vail High School, a prereading and premath response is administered to determine the students' proficiencies in these two areas. Data is shared with all teachers, administrators, and school counselor to determine ILP for student learning and placement into subject areas. At the end of the school year, students are given a post-test in the areas of reading and math to determine proficiency.

Standards-Based Student Learning: Instruction

All teachers modified and delivered instruction to address student needs. Differentiated instruction was utilized as the methodology that blends a variety of instructional strategies. The Vail High School staff provided differentiated content focusing on knowledge and skills, differentiated process focusing on performance tasks, and differentiated products focusing on the outcome(s) of student lesson(s). Teachers adapt and modify curriculum to accommodate students with justified sporadic attendance and reinstatement.

Reflective Practices:
Perspectives of Multi-Unicultural School
Leaders

Vail High School has implemented and piloted an online career-pathway initiative, Road Trip Nation, to enhance standards-based instruction and career pathways for students. Vail High School is one of three recognized model continuation high schools in the state of California to pilot Road Trip Nation this school year, 2009–2010. Road Trip Nation is an alternative online program that explores jobs, careers, life opportunities, choices, and goals that students may come to explore, understand, and fully appreciate. The Road Trip Nation initiative has invited Vail High School to continue with the generous grant. All training, materials, and support for the implementation of the program are at no cost to Vail High School and the Montebello Unified School District. Additional information may be found at www.roadtripnation.org.

Vail High School began to implement and pilot the principles of the Drucker Institute

Dr. Paul A. Rodríguez & Dr. Roberto F. Casas

(www.druckerla.org). The Drucker-in-High-Schools Program includes the following:

Cultivating a sense of social responsibility
Teaching management and leadership skills
Developing relationships with community leaders
Sharing a valuable self-management tool to guide future school and work plans
Creating a positive impact in the local community

Vail High School has worked with the city of Commerce librarian, Sonia Bautista, to increase the number of books available for the students' checkout and students' interest in reading. Sonia Bautista, a young adult librarian, works for the City of Commerce Public Library. With grant money, Sonia Bautista visited Vail High School to interact with and read to the students. This involved twenty students during the student lunch period for over three months.

Reflective Practices:
Perspectives of Multi-Unicultural School Leaders

Assessment and Accountability

Using core curriculum and a myriad of instruction materials that meet standards-based goals, teachers created and collectively developed midterm and benchmark assessments as part of Vail High School's formative assessment strand. Data generated from summative assessments was analyzed and utilized as an important part of Vail High School's accountability component. EZ Grade Pro and TeleParent progress reports were an integral part of Vail High School's accountability component. The attendance data was monitored schoolwide as well as by each student. Students became owners of their own attendance and academic success. Students were consistently made aware and encouraged to maintain attendance. In so doing, students addressed the importance of classroom attendance for enhanced academic progress.

Culture and Support for Student Personal, Social, Career, and Academic Growth

Administration and Vail's counselor regularly met with students and developed a course plan to encourage meeting graduation requirements and career goals. Progress reports are sent to parents on an ongoing basis to encourage parent support for student personal, social, career pathways, and academic growth. The district support is now evident for addressing the needs of chronically absent Vail High School students through the School Attendance Review Board (SARB) process.

Vail High School established two college career-job expos (fall and spring) that provided information and dialogue opportunities for parents, staff, students, and community to select a career pathway.

Reflective Practices:
Perspectives of Multi-Unicultural School Leaders

In addition, the expos increased parent participation with Vail High School, embracing the important parental-involvement component. Vail High School established a new, quarterly student-parent intake/enrollment for students entering Vail High School. Consequently, the quarterly orientation for student-parent has addressed Vail High School's overall exemplary programs for student personal, social, career pathways, and academic growth and success. Students and parents come to understand all the essential components that designate Vail High School as a model continuation high school.

Vail High School was recognized on May 2, 2010, at the state of California conference by the California Continuation Education Association for their exemplary program: College, Career, and Citizenship Program. The exemplary program enabled students to reflect on their own participatory *citizenship in our society. With the exemplary program recognition, Vail High School established and maintained a positive working relationship with Cal SOAP (California Student Opportunity and Access Program). Cal SOAP, throughout the year, planned and provided Vail High School seniors the opportunities to visit and tour local public and private universities and junior college campuses at no cost to the school and school district. Cal SOAP transported senior students to local colleges for entrance assessment tests and the fall 2010 matriculation/registration.*

Progress Critical Areas: Action Plan Impact Quality of Student Learning: API (Academic Performance Index)

2005	2006	2007	2008	2009		
383	597	660	520	607	2005–2009 +224	2008–2009 +87

Reflective Practices:
Perspectives of Multi-Unicultural School Leaders

				Growth	Growth

The Analysis of API Performance Data

The Academic Performance Index (API) data generated by the state department of education is the cornerstone of the Public Schools Accountability Act. This numeric index ranges from 200 to 1000. Eight hundred is the state performance target. Analysis of five data points, 2005 to 2009, indicated a tremendous growth of 224 points for the students served at Vail High School. Since Vail High School's accreditation visit in 2007, Vail High School has continued to work on programs and strategies to yield growth increments as the school monitored and adjusted programmatic strengths and needs as indicated by the state of California.

The API's evolving indicator weights that have moved into the direction of emphasizing assessment of state-adopted

Dr. Paul A. Rodríguez & Dr. Roberto F. Casas

content standards have influenced the school's priorities in staff development, schoolwide individual progress strategies, and support programs. Vail High School's API scores increased by eighty-seven points from 2008 to 2009 despite a prior year dip. Vail High School attributed the tremendous growth to the WASC input of the monitoring and adjusting strand of the schoolwide action plan as the administration and staff implemented innovative programs for Vail High School.

The faculty and administration collaboratively navigated the schoolwide programs, the implementation and enhancement of standards-based curriculum, and instruction strands that encouraged a crystal focus that positively impacted the student performance at Vail High School. Because of the Public Schools Accountability Act, Vail High School generated annual data to address the Alternative Schools Accountability Model (ASAM). Students' school

Reflective Practices:
Perspectives of Multi-Unicultural School Leaders

performance measures are based on multiple indicators that assess the schools ability to serve high-risk students.

Indicator number 6: Attendance has been measured by Vail High School over time. As part of the school's progress report, Vail High School has posted discernible gains in attendance since the last WASC six-year review in 2007. The following table provides a breakdown of the attendance indicator over a period of three years.

Vail High School Attendance

2006–2007	2007–2008	2008–2009	
70%	78%	90.29% (December, 2009)	Growth 2006–2009 +20.29%

Dr. Paul A. Rodríguez & Dr. Roberto F. Casas

Indicator number 9: Reading achievement was based on data for 2008–2009 on the student-level results of a prepost reading assessment (Performance Assessment Services). Seventy-nine students were tested (pretest) and 62 percent yielded growth results (post-test).

Additional Action Plan Areas Addressed

The continued data disaggregation embraced the quality of educational decisions for the students at Vail High School. The implementation of course mapping, student transcripts, test data, and student attendance were the primary tools for success at Vail High School. Vail High School's website was re-created and updated to increase communication with parents, students, and community stakeholders.

During the three years, the Vail High School principal retired, and a newly appointed principal, Dr. Paul A. Rodriguez,

Reflective Practices:
Perspectives of Multi-Unicultural School Leaders

joined the Vail High School team in October of 2007. Dr. Rodriguez continued to target the resources needed to further the goals of student achievement. Despite significant budget challenges, Dr. Rodriguez went the extra steps to continue to build a community of lifelong learners, a positive and safe learning environment, and encourage offering Vail High School students the latest in curriculum and instruction enhancements.

Strategies and Considerations

The successes at Vail High School were attributed to the transparency for open communication, trust, collaboration, and reflection for all interested stakeholders who visited Vail High School. The common ground for all the stakeholders focused on the sincerelness and dedication of the entire staff and administration to help all students achieve their academic, person,

Dr. Paul A. Rodríguez & Dr. Roberto F. Casas

social, and career goals in our democratic society.

Chapter 9
A Multi-unicultural Reflection: Music and the Arts

A handbook on cultural dances was developed for the elementary school grades four to six in June of 1994. The lesson was produced as a play, called A Blast Through the Past, and included songs in Spanish and English, one hundred twenty students from various cultural backgrounds, two large choirs, and the selected, secular Mexican regional dance "Las Chiapanecas." The handbook enhanced the elementary school curriculum by providing the teacher with directions and explanations on how to teach students selected secular Mexican regional dances. The teacher was provided with historical explanations for each dance, as well as illustrations for costumes. In addition, the teacher was provided with information on

Reflective Practices:
Perspectives of Multi-Unicultural School
Leaders

the history of Mexican regional music and dance, status of multicultural education, aspects of multicultural education, theoretical foundations of the arts, educational value of dance, multicultural perspectives of dance, multicultural aspects of dance curriculum, and recommendations. Lastly, a list of definition of terms was provided for understanding. The concept of multi-uniculturalism was coined by the author in June of 1994 and is defined and explained.

Introduction

Within a multicultural educational framework, cultural diversity is seen as a positive reality in the United States and requires a global approach for instruction. All peoples, nations, and cultures contribute and grow in a culturally diverse nation and world. It is within our historical heritage to acknowledge and respect each individual regardless of ethnicity, race, religion, sex,

Dr. Paul A. Rodríguez & Dr. Roberto F. Casas

and socioeconomic status, physical or mental ability. All leaders and educators must recognize and embrace the integrity of all group cultures.

Dance, the most ancient of arts, has been an integral part of religious customs and rituals. It is important to the socialization process in civilization. Dance can make a significant contribution to the curriculum with human development and expression. The California Visual and Performing Arts Framework assert, "The dance experience is an ideal instrument for developing and enriching bilingual and multicultural programs because dance is a nonverbal medium."

Participation in dances of other cultures enables the student to experience feelings, sensations, and ideas associated with those cultures. Students can sense the rich contributions of the multiethnic and multicultural groups, past and present, that

Reflective Practices:
Perspectives of Multi-Unicultural School Leaders

make the American society. Saxe (1989) states that,

I have pointed out that democracy in our nation serves a pluralistic society, but that this society needs a cultural currency to function efficiently. Harmony is found in diversity, not sameness. Likewise, democracy is a result of collective sharing among willing participants seeking substance and unity.

The very complexity and diversity within our American society coheres for the inclusion of multiculturalism in dance education curriculum. Many dances draw upon dances of other cultures. An appreciation of the similarities and distinctions of various cultures is gained through the study of folk dance. Dance reflects the personality and temperament of a people that gives dance its lasting appeal.

Likewise, researchers inform us that that the brain operates on an emotional bias system. Information that is perceived by the learner as helpful, interesting, rewarding (Hart 1975, Sagan 1977), and or gamey is eventually processed by the brain. In short, we learn what we want to learn. Cognitive functioning is determined by the emotional state of the learner (Galyean 1981). Many dance movements can signify universal shared meanings. Viewed as a universal language, symbolizing through dance furthers the child's knowledge of the world and its diverse cultures. Exposure to dance helps children understand and appreciate their own culture and the culture of others. Subsequently, dance constitutes a mean for helping students learn how to live in peace, harmony, and mutual respect in a complex, pluralistic society.

Status of Multicultural Education

The status of multicultural education has become a very important factor in today's educational system. Our educational system must provide an avenue for children

Reflective Practices:
Perspectives of Multi-Unicultural School
Leaders

to develop into productive and contributing citizens. There is legitimacy for diversity and multicultural education at all levels of the curriculum of instruction (Baptiste 1979). Hollins (1982) asserted the need for the creation of a multicultural theory of learning. Accordingly, Hollins states that Piaget's theory did not allow for cultural differences in the onset of the various stages. It was found that most other learning theories also lacked a multicultural or cross-cultural dimension. Therefore, it is important to formulate a multicultural learning theory that would take into account the cultural bias inherent in most related research.

Individuality and culture are interrelated. Multicultural education must view learners as not only contributors to society and the educational system, but also to themselves (Francis 1992). A multi-unicultural perspective must be integrated into the educational system. A multi-unicultural concept allows individuals to first and simultaneously comprehend and embrace their own unique beliefs, values, traditions, language, customs, relationships, experiences, and physical environment prior to understanding and acknowledging other cultures. This perspective involves the individual's conscious and subconscious reflections and memories of past, present, and future events into a collective reflection of who and how others and themselves perceive them. Today, this is known as intracultural diversity. Our American educational system has not always promoted personal oneness and identity, but has advocated a Eurocentric orientation of losing the majority of one's own culture through the blending of another. The history of our American educational system has at times ignored the cultural diversity of society (Francis 1992).

Aspects of Multicultural Education

Reflective Practices:
Perspectives of Multi-Unicultural School Leaders

Our school environments should enhance the students' emotional well being and positive self-esteem. In spite of the fact that prejudices cannot be eliminated, much can be done to make the school environment a better one for all students. Cultural awareness activities can involve school personnel, students, and the community members. These activities can sensitize people to the needs and feelings of others. The California History Social Science Framework and the Visual and Performing Arts Framework for California public schools both promote the importance of integrating a multicultural perspective into our instructional curriculum. Dance students can sense the rich contributions of the multiethnic and multicultural groups, past and present, which make up the American heritage. Teachers are called to "acknowledge that the history of community, state, region, nation and world must reflect the experience of all people from different racial, religious and ethnic groups."

Multicultural Education Definition

*Cultural diversity is seen as a positive reality in the United States.
Cultural diversity is seen as a valuable resource to be preserved and utilized.
Cultural diversity and cultural differences are a valuable and vital force in the development of our society.
Acknowledges the belief in our constitution for the respect of each individual regardless of ethnicity, race, religion, sex, socioeconomic status, physical or mental ability
Strives to blend affective and cognitive growth
Within the requirements of national unity, acknowledges the integrity of group cultures*

Multicultural Education Goals

Reflective Practices:
Perspectives of Multi-Unicultural School Leaders

To develop a positive self-image in order to understand one's own culture and develop an appreciation for the culture of others

To develop an understanding of one's own value systems, cultures, customs, and histories, as well as others outside of oneself

To develop an appreciation of individual and cultural differences

To provide a base for productive participation in one or more cultures

To develop a desire to contribute to and grow in a culturally diverse nation and world

To develop a respect for freedom and dignity of others and to accept the responsibility for sustaining and increasing the institutions of all people in a multicultural and interdependent society in order to contribute to a greater freedom for all (Chapman 1983)

Kniep (1989) noted that instructors should give students a basic knowledge of the values of their own cultures and society.

Likewise, students should be encouraged to examine the values of others and see the commonality and diversity among people. Saxe (1989) concurred that in order to have a harmony in our society, instructors need to look to the diversity of individuals to realize collective sharing and unity.

I point out that democracy in our nation serves a pluralistic society; this society needs a cultural currency to function efficiently. Educators at all levels need to seek the common ground, to examine the roots and history of the foundational studies as well as the social studies in order to harmonize their positions in the curriculum. (p. 40)

Theoretical Foundations of the Arts

There are several theoretical groundworks for the developmental learning of children. Careful investigation of the various developmental theories can lead to genuine ways of traversing behaviors and situations.

*Reflective Practices:
Perspectives of Multi-Unicultural School
Leaders*

The examination of these forms of theories can manifest an opportunity for cogitation and comprehension of experiences. Therefore, educational practice becomes a circumstance that enhances learning for both students and instructor.

Intellectual Development

Through the clinical researcher Jean Piaget, we have learned that children think differently and progress through a qualitative path to maturity. Children of school age make the transition from the preoperational stage of development (ages 2–6) to the concrete, operational state (ages 7–11). Within the preoperational stage, children are able to form mental images. Children are capable to think of and imagine objects and events not physically present. While in the concrete operational period, children become increasingly competent of mental actions that are reversible, relying on concrete

Dr. Paul A. Rodríguez & Dr. Roberto F. Casas

objects that are physically present. Consequently, reinforcing the mental growth of children adheres to learning environments that provide for hands-on activities and interesting objects that promote real-life experiences. The experiences and activities become the basis for the children's stored mental images and mental representations. Integrating the arts—such as drama, music, art, storytelling, poems, movement, and dance—into the curriculum provides opportunities to integrate mental representation symbolically for the child. The student's intellectual development is increased in a motivating, interesting, and fun way.

According to Piaget (1985), children learn new knowledge through active discovery based on their experiences and their immediate levels of cognitive development. Henceforth, children need to participate in activities that provide opportunities for expressive play, exploration, and discovery. Adler (1968) stated the following:

Reflective Practices:
Perspectives of Multi-Unicultural School
Leaders

Of all the organs with which a child attempts the conquest of the world, the sense organs are the most important in the determination of the essential relationships to the world in which he lives. It is through the sense organs that one constructs one's cosmic picture. (p. 45)

Gardner (1983) developed new theories of intelligence. Gardner identifies several intelligences that include the following:

Linguistic: the ability to use language to excite, please, convinces, stimulate, or convey information
Musical: the ability to enjoy, performs, or composes a musical piece
Logical-mathematical: the ability to explore patterns, categories, and relationships by manipulating objects or symbols and to experience in a controlled, orderly way

Dr. Paul A. Rodríguez & Dr. Roberto F. Casas

Spatial: the ability to perceive and mentally manipulate a form or object, to perceive and crease tension, balance, and composition in a visual or spatial display
Bodily kinesthetic: the ability to use fine and gross motor skills in sports, the performing arts, or arts and crafts production
Interpersonal: the ability to understand and get along with others
Intrapersonal: the ability to gain access to and understand one's inner feelings, dreams, and ideas
Naturalist: the ability to recognize and categorize plants, animals, and other objects in nature
Existential: the ability for sensitivity and capacity to tackle deep questions about human existence such as the meaning of life, why do we die, and how did we get here

Our educational system has, in the past, focused on two intelligences, those being linguistic and logical-mathematical. Gardner (1983) defines intelligence as those activities that create products or the ability to solve problems that are greatly valued within one or more cultural backgrounds. Accepting this redefinition of intelligence expands our views of the arts and its function in school curriculum and environments.

Social Development

Vygotsky (1978) asserted that higher mental functions are formed through social interactions and result in the transmission of culture. Interactions with other individuals help the child understand their own feelings and the feelings of others. In so doing, through the interpersonal interaction and contact with various objects and individuals, the child will achieve fundamental prerequisites for aesthetic practice. As Gardner (1973) asserted,

Development of the self through imitation and communication is an unconscious as *well as a conscious process, and, a person's sense of self, his identity, to use the current parlance, is an enormously complex and subtle phenomenon. (p. 95)*

Therefore, if social interactions are important, "then the classroom environment must stimulate discussions about literature, favorite paintings and photographs, and most-loved music" (Cecil and Lauritzen 1994, p. 5). The arts encourage participation and interaction where every child can contribute and discover. As Gardner (1973) enunciated,

Indeed, if the arts involve communication of information about subjective experience, the initial manifestation of such communication may be crucial; "truth" or "genuineness" in works of art may reflect the sense of well-being and veridicality paramount in encounters with human beings. (Gardner 1973, p. 97)

Reflective Practices:
Perspectives of Multi-Unicultural School Leaders

Teachers and parents can help children develop their artistic creativity and understanding with exposure to artists and their works. Art might become more real and less remote. Gardner (1982) believed that if children in the early grades could follow a creation of a painting from beginning to end, they might better understand the differences between an object and its representation.

Indeed, if children are left to acquire understanding on their own, the whole domain of the arts may remain for them as distant as a star, as mysterious as the speaker of a dead language. (Gardner 1982, p. 109)

Emotional Development

Gardner (1990) suggested that there is at least five different kinds of knowledge that any individual who grows up in a schooled environment must ultimately attempt to

Dr. Paul A. Rodríguez & Dr. Roberto F. Casas

master and integrate. Children during their first years of life obtain a large amount of knowledge by virtue of their interactions with physical objects and with other persons. Much of this knowledge is acquired through sensory perceptions and motor interactions and is developed through the stimulation of these faculties. There is an understanding "about the predictable behavior of objects in the environment, the motivations and intentions of other persons, the physical appearance of familiar entities, and other universally accessible forms of information" (Gardner 1990, p. 26).

Within the second stage of knowledge, individuals begin to use and master the most widely available symbol systems of their culture, for example words, pictures, gestures, musical patterns, personal relationships, and the like. The materialization of these cognitive inclinations is facilitated by rich and varied exposure (Cecil and Lauritzen 1994, p. 6).

***Reflective Practices:
Perspectives of Multi-Unicultural School
Leaders***

Around the age of five to seven, children begin to display signs that they wish to employ various kinds of notational systems, which are usually termed notational systems (Vygotsky 1978). These notational systems have evolved in literate cultures in order to refer especially to the first-order symbol systems. Gardner (1990) explained:

Hence, written language refers to oral language; written numerical systems denote oral and sensorial known quantitative information; written musical notational systems capture the defining features of music valued in the culture; and various codes, graphs, maps and the like capture other important symbolic and intuitive lessons. (p. 6)

Many individuals will proceed to develop their own forms of notation, but it is probable that such systems would not develop without the prior existence of model cultural notations.

Dr. Paul A. Rodríguez & Dr. Roberto F. Casas

The fourth form of knowledge is the mastery of various concepts, principles, and formal bodies of knowledge that researchers, scholars, and reflective human beings have discovered, invented, and/or codified over the centuries. Gardner (1990) believed that without formal schooling, there is very little probability that the average person in society would be exposed to them and virtually no chance that they would master them.
Lastly, the fifth form of knowledge, Gardner (1990) identified as "skilled knowledge." All cultures shelter a collection of crafts, disciplines, and practices that need mastery by some individuals in order for the knowledge of that society to be passed on to the next generation.

Human development must embrace all the various aspects of experiences that uniquely constitute that whole person. Educational systems often maintain that the arts are solely opportunities for self-expression rather than means of reaching intellectual development. The integration of the arts into every educational curriculum fosters the uniqueness and multi-uniculturalism of each child. Children make sense of their world when educational experiences are focused on their individual styles of learning and discovery.

Educational Value of Dance

Dance has been a way of expression and sensitivity throughout human existence. Children are natural movers and full of energy that startles us with their grace and beauty of spontaneous movement play. Logan (1984, p. 37) believed that "what more fitting way for children to harness their energy and imagination than to give form to that movement expression—to dance?" All children should be given the opportunity to participate in dance regardless of their gender. As Stinson (1989) proclaimed, "Even more important, these exploratory experiences contribute to the life of every *child, not just those little girls who dream of wearing a tutu" (p. 205).*

Traditionally, dance as an art form is one of the least understood. Sparshott (1990) asserted "dance is in a curious situation in the public consciousness of the arts" (p. 77). Heretofore, "dance is an art form that is characterized by use of the human body as a vehicle of expression" (Overby 1992, p. 1). No special equipment is needed, just the ability to move. Until recently, dance was taught mainly as an activity in the physical education curriculum. It is now recognized as an "art form comparable to music, drams, and visual arts, equally worthy of study" (Carter 1984, p. 295). Children demystify the aesthetic dimensions of dance movement through sound and movement. When children know what is involved in making and performing dance, it enables them to look at it with sharpened perception and insight.

Reflective Practices:
Perspectives of Multi-Unicultural School Leaders

Although dance is an eloquent art form, however, a nonverbal one does not lend itself to the normal modes of cognitive investigation. For this reason, students do not gain ready access to dance, especially in educational systems that value more linear approaches to learning. Logan (1984) maintained that,

Like the other arts, dance gives us access to a nonverbal metaphoric dimension of experiences, one that has to be experiences to be understood; and yet, once children go beyond the early elementary grades, this mode of learning is neglected and ignored. (p. 38)

When dance movement activities and sensations of moving are associated to the expressive and imaginative elements of the mover, dance commences. With dance appreciation, the child heightens their kinesthetic awareness, bodily intelligence,

Dr. Paul A. Rodríguez & Dr. Roberto F. Casas

and sharpens their perception of movement as a dimension of aesthetic experience.

Multicultural Perspective of Dance

Dance has become a foremost force of expression among minorities in the United States. Trujillo (1979) states that dance serves the purpose of ethnic unity, identity, and cultural expression (p. 1). Yet, Americans know very little about dance. The culturally literate Americans know absolutely nothing about dancing or the dance, except that there is something called ballet. Sparshott (1990) enunciated that "he knows about that because his granddaughter wants to grow to be a ballerina. And, oh yes—didn't there used to be that couple who were in movies back in the thirties?" (p. 74).

The United States is not an effective cultural community. The most important

***Reflective Practices:
Perspectives of Multi-Unicultural School
Leaders***

goal in any cultural community is to provide a core of assumptions about the range of what a person is expected to know. Within that community, there should be an educational system that supplies every citizen with the means to mastering that range. Olneck (1990) stated that,

People of color have argued that what is important to their concerns and self-esteem has been relatively unimportant to the dominant society who believe that they alone should decide whose knowledge is to be counted and who's is to be disqualified. (p. 35)

Yet, the concept of ethnic diversity is not new or specific. Multicultural education has become an increasingly important factor in the education of our nation's children. Possibly, educators are realizing that it is important to develop multicultural curricula and teaching strategies and that the history of America's multicultural inheritance is unfinished. Marich (1991) protested that people of color have angrily pointed their finger at "Eurocentric curricular offerings and the dominant 'left-brain' way of knowing the world" (p. 4). We must formulate new multicultural education. In so doing, students can explore their peers' complex cultural dimensions.

Multicultural education must perceive the learner as contributor to society, the educational system, and themselves. It can focus on individuality and enhance the child's freedom to enrich and design their lives. Multicultural education is capable of measuring diversity as a force for human emancipation and facilitating dignity among groups (Rosengren, Wiley, and Wiley 1983).

Multicultural Aspects of Dance Curriculum

Studies show that the number of ethnic minority children is increasing. Teachers

Reflective Practices:
Perspectives of Multi-Unicultural School Leaders

need to be versed in multicultural education to teach about it and at the same time to be sensitive to the educational needs of minority children. The California Visual and Performing Arts Framework recognizes the importance of incorporating a multicultural perspective throughout the visual and performing arts curriculum.

The teacher is able to illustrate how basic American dance education relates to all cultural forms of dance. In fact, students, through their own dance work, can make creative contributions to their changing culture. (p. 31)

Within a multicultural education framework, cultural diversity is seen as a positive reality in the United States and a valuable resource that must be served and utilized. Likewise, cultural diversity and cultural differences are a valuable vital force in the development of our society. Our historical heritage acknowledges the belief in our constitution for respect of each individual regardless of ethnicity, race, religion, sex, and socioeconomic status, physical or mental ability and strives to blend affective and cognitive growth. Within the requirements of national unity, educators acknowledge the integrity of group cultures (Francis 1992).

The goals of the multicultural education curriculum have been based on a developed, positive self-esteem, an appreciation for one's culture and the culture of others. In addition, it develops an appreciation of individual and cultural differences and provides a base for productive participation in one or more cultures. It develops a desire to contribute to growth in a culturally diverse nation and world. It develops a respect for freedom and dignity of others to accept the responsibility for sustaining and increasing the institutions of all people in a multicultural and interdependent society to contribute to a greater freedom for all.

Reflective Practices:
Perspectives of Multi-Unicultural School
Leaders

Similarly, it offers a large spectrum of choices in careers, choices involving culturally evolved lifestyles, which are based on each individual's desires, aspirations, and capabilities.

Schwartz (1991) stated that the complexity and diversity within our American society adhere for the inclusion of multiculturalism in dance education curriculum.

Much of modern dance draws upon dances of other cultures, and through a study of folk dance, an appreciation of the similarities and distinctions of various cultures is also gained. Dance may be used as a one of many windows to the history, religions and customs of people. (p. 46)

The status of dance education is that at least fifteen states have developed dance curriculum guidelines, including California. However, except for North Carolina, no state has mandated that the guidelines be implemented (Gingrasso and Stinson 1989). Howe (1989) affirmed that "teachers must be introduced to and receive training in dance so that they can include it appropriately within their lesson plans" (p. 46).

Many of the curriculum guides contain specific content, goals, objectives, and limited measurable outcomes for such areas as the following:

Dance techniques for social, modern, and ethnic dance
Aesthetic perception
Kinesthetic sense
Creative expression
Choreography
Dance criticism

While many cultures have embraced dance as an integral part of religious customs and rituals, Cecil and Lauritzen (1994) asserted that dance serves no significance in

***Reflective Practices:
Perspectives of Multi-Unicultural School
Leaders***

American culture. Children are exposed to the role of audience or, at the most part, an amateur performance or two (p. 109).

Dance movements can signify universal shared meanings. Symbolizing through dance, as in language, furthers the child's knowledge of the world and its diverse cultures. Dance's interwoven exchange between motor and cognitive activities makes it a unique way of accepting and formulating knowledge.

In considering a wholesome dance curriculum, educators should consider the following:

Exposure to dance helps children understand and appreciate their own culture and the cultures of others.
The basic components of dance are pivotal concepts in many other curricular areas and can therefore be integrated with and enhance mathematics, social sciences, and the language arts.

Dr. Paul A. Rodríguez & Dr. Roberto F. Casas

Dance provides an intuitive, affective mode of knowing through kinesthetic expression. Dance as an avenue of self-expression affords an alternative way of being successful for ELD learners and other children who do not or cannot respond successfully to verbal instruction. (Cecil and Lauritzen 1994, p. 109)

In so doing, children will be able to demonstrate through movement that dance is a form of communication and that the variety of movement comes from the uniqueness of each individual is expression. The student should develop a knowledge and appreciation of our multi-unicultural dance heritage and recognize the dance as a universal language in world cultures.

Strategies and Considerations

As our nation moves from a majority of Anglo-Americans to one of multiethnic cultural diversity, it becomes increasingly

Reflective Practices:
Perspectives of Multi-Unicultural School Leaders

important to promote a multi-unicultural educational program in schools. What makes our nation strong and unique is our diversity of people. Increasing the awareness of our multicultural dance heritage strengthens our future in an ever-changing cosmos.

Students should be taught in ways that enable them to develop knowledge, skills, and good attitudes. There needs to be a social environment, climate, or culture that supports all aspects of learning. Equally, there needs to be a sense of community where mutual sharing among professionals and students is strengthened and active individual group cooperation, collaboration by both professionals and students, is encouraged. The integration of dance education and all the arts provides a unique and needed diversity within the school setting by involving the child's physical as well as the mental processes.

Dr. Paul A. Rodríguez & Dr. Roberto F. Casas

Gardner argues that there is both a biological and cultural basis for the multiple intelligences. Neurobiological research indicates that learning is an outcome of the modifications in the synaptic connections between cells. Primary elements of different types of learning are found in particular areas of the brain where corresponding transformations have occurred. Consequently, various types of learning result in synaptic connections in different areas of the brain. For instance, injury to the Broca's area of the brain will result in the loss of one's ability to verbally communicate using proper syntax. Nevertheless, this injury will not remove the patient's understanding of correct grammar and word usage.

Gardner (1983) argued that culture also plays a large role in the development of the intelligences. All societies value different types of intelligences. The cultural value placed upon the ability to perform certain tasks provides the motivation to

***Reflective Practices:
Perspectives of Multi-Unicultural School
Leaders***

become skilled in those areas. Thus, while particular intelligences might be highly evolved in many people of one culture, those same intelligences might not be as developed in the individuals of another. Teachers should structure the presentation of material in a style, which engages most or all the intelligences. By activating a wide assortment of intelligences, teaching can facilitate a deeper understanding of the subject material.

Schools have often sought to help students develop a sense of accomplishment and self-confidence. While not all students may be verbally or mathematically gifted, children may have an expertise in other areas such as music, spatial relations, or interpersonal knowledge. Approaching and assessing learning in this manner allows a wider range of students to successfully participate in classroom learning.

Dr. Paul A. Rodríguez & Dr. Roberto F. Casas

Definitions of Terms

aesthetic: Is the search and appreciation for beauty

appositional: Describes the type of cognition proper to the right hemisphere in contrast to the common use by neurologists of propositional for the left hemisphere (Bogen 1973)

co-operative learning: Is a process that enables the student to listen to others, evaluate the problem, and make decisions for the common good of the group. It develops negotiating skills to work toward solutions that are the goals of the group (Geiger and Rodríguez 1993).

***Reflective Practices:
Perspectives of Multi-Unicultural School
Leaders***

culture: Is created by people in social environments and systems composed of unique beliefs, values, traditions, language, customs, technology, and institutions as a way of meeting basic human needs; shaped by their own physical environments and contact with other cultures (Kniep 1979).

ethnic group: Is relating to a group of people who are bound together by language, religious, or cultural ties (Banks 1984).

ethnic minority group: Is an ethnic group with several distinguishing characteristics. Although an ethnic minority group, like an ethnic group, shares a common culture, a historic tradition, and a sense of peoplehood, it also has unique physical and/or cultural characteristics that enable individuals who belong to other ethnic groups to identify its members easily, often for discriminatory purposes. Ethnic minority groups also tend to be a numerical minority and to exercise little political and economic power (Banks 1984).

hands-on experience: Is a process that enables the student to listen to others, evaluate the problem, and make decisions for the common good of the group. It develops negotiating skills to work toward solutions that are the goals of the group (Geiger and Rodríguez 1993).

left brain: Refers to the left hemisphere of the brain that deals with verbal, analytical, rational, logical, and linear functioning. Bogen (1973) called this mode "propositional" to avoid only value judgments about which hemisphere is superior.

multicultural education: Is the teaching of cultures that differ from the dominant culture in ethically, race, language, or appearance (Gezi 1981).

Reflective Practices:
Perspectives of Multi-Unicultural School
Leaders

multi-unicultural(ism): Is the concept that prior to understanding and acknowledging other cultures, individuals must first comprehend and embrace their own unique beliefs, values, traditions, language, relationships, socioeconomic status, customs, and physical environment. Simultaneously, the individual's reflections of past, present, and future events and relationships influence how they perceive themselves and others and how they react and interact with other individuals and events. This phenomenon happens within the individual, consciously or subconsciously, in every event, and within their entire relationships encountered. The individual's multi-unicultural behaviors to events and relationships may be verbal or nonverbal. The more the individual reflects on their own culture, customs, traditions, the more they are capable of understanding the similarities and dissimilarities of other individuals. The outcome is a greater understanding of themselves and how the individual functions in their surroundings and society (researcher, Rodríguez 1994).

nonverbal: Is the human expression of ideas and feelings without oral speech or written symbols

pluralism: Is a concept in which different groups maintain their individuality while functioning effectively in society (Weaver 1989)

propositional: Categorizes the linear, logical, analytic "if-then" processing of the left hemisphere in contrast to appositional thought. Propositional is a mental process highly receptive to codified knowledge (Bogen 1973).

right brain: Refers to the right hemisphere of the brain that deals with visual, holistic, nonverbal, emotions, and movement functioning. Bogen (1973) called this mode "appositional" to avoid any value judgments

Reflective Practices:
Perspectives of Multi-Unicultural School
Leaders

about which hemisphere is superior. When both hemispheres work together, the capacity for two minds exists.

Dr. Paul A. Rodríguez & Dr. Roberto F. Casas

Chapter 10
California Common Core Standards: Concerns/ Considerations for Alternative Education Students, Schools, and Programs

The political ramifications of mandated "high-stakes" student testing and assessment have become a fundamental reality, as has many other irresistible movements that have swept over our nations educational policies and legislation. Much has been written about educational inequities, dating back to the Coleman Report, almost 50 years ago. Educational inequities are part of the realities of our American culture. The educational agenda has become political folly for politicians and lawmakers. High stakes assessment and standardized assessments reflect a revised ideology for accountability. Defenders of standardized testing do not try to deny the fact that it forces schools to reconfigure and realign the "written, taught and tested curriculum". In a personal interview with Dr. Paul Rodriguez, author and Assistant Professor, at Pacific Oaks College, School of Education, he stated: The problem, I have with California Common Core is, "one shoe" does not fit all. (Rodriguez, 2013).

The concept of "curriculum alignment" utilizing, core standards is an attempt at closing the "achievement gap" among racial minority students and their peers. The fact that a "one-size" fits all assessment does not provide for "equity", and is biased towards diverse learners. According to Freedman (1993), it seems that it is done deliberately because it offers policy makers "one of the few levers on the curriculum that they can control." (p.49)

The newest "policy window" in education are Common Core Standards which are mandated to ensure a consistent, clear, concise definition of what students are required to learn and what is expected of them to prepare for success in post-secondary education or career preparation and life itself. The impact of high-stakes accountability on "At-Risk" and poor performing students is rarely taken into consideration when the development and/or implementation of accountability systems are designed. According to Michael Fullan,

I would hypothesize that the greater the emphasis on academic achievement through high-stakes accountability, the greater the gap becomes between *advantaged and disadvantaged students. The main reason for this is that poor performing students do not need more pressure; they need greater attachment to the school and motivation to want to learn. Pressure by itself in this situation actually de-motivates poor performing students."*

As a former Alternative School and Court School principal, I have come to realize that high-stakes testing is as about as important for 'At-risk" and poor performing students as it is for them listening to Mozart on their favorite Oldies or R & B radio station. One would think that when officials sit down to formulate an education policy, they would begin with the "end in mind", and they would start by agreeing on some broad outlines of what students ought to know that should include academic, social, and emotional considerations. By requiring, that

Dr. Paul A. Rodríguez & Dr. Roberto F. Casas

"ALL" students will rise to Common Core Standards is assuming all students are as "common" as one another are without considering their vast diversity. The Common Core standards do not provide for differentiation for special need students, English learners or the "gang" student being schooled in California Youth Authority. The idea that special education students, English language learners, and "At-risk' students are all the same common learners, lacks the focus of ensuring educational equity. In a recent article published by, the Regional Equity Assistance Center on Implementation of Common Core State Standards, stated,

"We have entered the sixth generation facing many challenges. Chief among them are the persistent achievement gaps between different ethnic and economic groups; ongoing disproportionality in the

***Reflective Practices:
Perspectives of Multi-Unicultural School
Leaders***

student groups represented in special education, in gifted and talented program, and the disciplinary categories; unacceptable school dropout rates; and continued low college-going and college completion rates for students of color, ELL students, students with disabilities, and economically disadvantaged students. If the Common Core is to achieve their promise of success for all students, they must be implemented in ways that can directly address and resolve these critical issues. The kind of high- quality education envisioned in the Common Core cannot remain a privilege reserved for only some students". Obviously, school administrators, educators, politicians, school boards and decision makers at all levels of the educational systems should start, at the minimum, to examine, and discuss their systems, policies, procedures and practices that ask the following questions:

- ➤ *How does this (policy/system/practice/procedure) impact ALL learners, helping those considered "at-risk' to become "at-promise"?*
- ➤ *"Can we identify negative or adverse consequences for any identifiable population as a result of this system, policy, procedure, and practice? (Regional Equity Assistance centers…p.3)*
- ➤ *Going forward when developing systemic practices, policies, and procedures, what steps shall we take to avoid negative consequences by not considering impacts on "at-risk" students?*

Reflective Practices:
Perspectives of Multi-Unicultural School
Leaders

- *How do we assess our work to ensure high quality learning outcomes for all students?*

- *How do we embrace and engage our parents, stakeholders and families, and our community to collaborate with us in the decision making process on behalf of our students?*

Because standardized tests, high-stakes assessments and accountability are the "only games" in town, those of us in education will continue to hear words from policy makers to describe student performance expectations as " tough, competitive, world-class, measurable, standards, results and raise –the-bar."

Dr. Paul A. Rodríguez & Dr. Roberto F. Casas

As stated by David Sousa's <u>The Leadership Brain: How to Lead Todays's Schools More Effectively,</u> *he wrote,*

The standards movement resulted from continuing complaints from the media and legislators that American students were lagging behind students in the rest of the industrialized world. The curriculum was too lax and our country would not remain competitive unless students achieved more challenging and complex learning objectives. The approach proposed that content experts set high standards for students to achieve so they can be ready for the workplace in highly complex, changing world. Despite well-intentioned purpose of high standards, educational leaders need to ask the following questions:

Reflective Practices:
Perspectives of Multi-Unicultural School Leaders

How can outside experts know how difficult it is for students to achieve the new standards?

- *Does achieving higher academic standards equate with being more successful in the future workplace?*
- *Does setting higher standards result in improved teaching and learning?*
- *Does high-stakes testing program associated with standards divert too much time and resources to teaching for the test at the expense of other worthwhile curricular activities?*
- *Will pressure of such a high-stakes program associated with the standards provoke teachers to resort to "drill and kill' on just those concepts they believe will be on the test, and revert to didactic, lecture-centered approaches that are hardly brain compatible for most students?*

In retrospect, it seems obvious that

Dr. Paul A. Rodríguez & Dr. Roberto F. Casas

alternative education programs would have a "differentiated" assessment model by which students should be measured by; because of their "uncommon" style of learning. Well over 13 years ago in 2000, California passed legislative for an Alternative Schools Accountability Model (ASAM), as an alternative assessment to the Accountability Performance Index (API). This alternative schools accountability model no longer applies to alternative schools and programs, because they are not common schools. School systems should evaluate how "alternative education students and students "at-risk" are being served and assessed. With that in-mind, school districts must begin to "create an assessment culture", that attempts to provide for 'equity and equality', for all students, even those students that are considered to be "UNCOMMON" in their

Reflective Practices:
Perspectives of Multi-Unicultural School Leaders

learning styles. Common Core standards must be implemented with the idea of ensuring that every student achieves their highest potential. Coupled with sound alternative education strategies delivered to students, in meeting Common Core Standards; "at-risk" and alternative education students must be taught by highly qualified" teachers under the leadership of Multi-unicultural school leaders. (Casas, R & Rodriguez, P, 2012)

In my attempt to figure out why Common Core for all students is the new California norm; I can only think that our government wants all our students to conform to a Common Federal Standards system. In a book that speaks directly to Federal Standards conformity, I read the early work of Ellwood Patterson Cubberly, author of <u>Changing Conceptions of Education,</u> *where*

Dr. Paul A. Rodríguez & Dr. Roberto F. Casas

he attempts to provide the framework as to why ALL students (i.e. minority students, students of color, ELL students and at-risk students) must conform to American educational agendas (such as Common Core Standards). Cubberly stated the purpose of education is " to assimilate and amalgamate these people as part of our American race, and to implant in their children, so far as can be done, the Anglo-Saxon conception of righteousness, law and order, and popular government, and to awaken in them a reverence for our democratic institutions and for those things in our national life which we people hold to be abiding worth". (Cubberly, 1909)

Although Cubberly wrote this statement in 1909, the American educational system has not changed in the approach to student accountability or curriculum delivery. It seems Cubberly's words speaks volumes

Reflective Practices:
Perspectives of Multi-Unicultural School
Leaders

as to why standards have to be common and the thought as to why legislators want students to be assessed using the same federally recommended assessment tool.

In a recent online article in <u>EDUCATION WEEK</u> *(April 23, 2014),* <u>Resistance to Common Core Mounts,</u> *it states," The common Core has drawn criticism from both the political left and right, though much of it seems aimed not so much at what the standards say, but rather who drove the adoption of tests and accountability policies connected with them." Further the article states," At the same time, union leaders and other progressives in education in places like Maryland and New York state have be decrying what they see as lack of preparation and resources for teachers as the standards are carried out. These critics*

Dr. Paul A. Rodríguez & Dr. Roberto F. Casas

say states should delay the full impact of the common-core standards and tests on educators, students and schools."

The financial carrot waved in the faces of state lawmakers by the Federal Department of Education, did not require states to adopt the standards, but it did offer incentives through the federal Race to the Top initiative. The Feds have provided $360 million to two state consortia to develop assessments aligned with the standards. The problem is that the "Euro-centric" assessment is aligned with the standards and NOT with the cultural and linguistic learning styles of our diverse student population, specifically those "alternative education" students that are more focused on issues such as self-esteem, bullying and alternative learning styles. These "Uncommon" students are being assessed with Common-core standards, but are not

Reflective Practices:
Perspectives of Multi-Unicultural School Leaders

attending common or core school sites, but alternative settings.

Again as stated earlier, this political window is creating a political backlash in states such as Indiana, New York, Georgia and Tennessee. In direct admonition however, prominent advocates of the standards, from U.S. Chamber of Commerce to Florida Gov. Jeb Bush, a Republican, and Delaware Gov. Jack Markell, a Democrat have established and set-up, "myth-busting" sites and public relations campaigns to support the high stakes, common standards. According to Markell, " What we didn't expect was a lot of misinformation that would be spread around the country what these standards are, Markell further stated, "we have to invest the time and we have to invest the effort to make sure that the value of these

Dr. Paul A. Rodríguez & Dr. Roberto F. Casas

standards is communicated to people across the country".

It is this writer's belief that not only do we have to invest time and effort on the value of the standards, but we also have to value the diverse student population who will be assessed by the common-core. There needs to be an investment of "sweat equity" and effort to find out the various learning styles of our diverse student population in order to get the best results on the assessments. I argue that what you will not find is a "common core" of students that will all have the same learning style and test taking skills, to relate too or even pass the Common Core assessment.

In closing, I believe one of my former alternative education students summed it up the best, and provides credibility to my assertions, when I asked him what he

Reflective Practices:
Perspectives of Multi-Unicultural School
Leaders
thought about the new Common-Core Standards? He responded, "Common-Que?" (translated, common what?)

Dr. Paul A. Rodríguez & Dr. Roberto F. Casas

Chapter 11
**An Alternative Instructional Delivery Model: The Independent Study Program
Introduction**

"The great task of teachers as curriculum designs, then, is to move students from momentary interest or caprice, to consideration of the deeper mysteries revealed by their momentary concern."
(Schubert, W.H. 1994, p. 29).

<u>Why I chose this topic</u>

***Reflective Practices:
Perspectives of Multi-Unicultural School
Leaders***

The reason I chose this topic is my interest in alternative education delivery models. My professional background and experience has been dominated by my work in alternative education and in education of students "at-risk."

My autobiography has led me to internalize my vocation and to re-think where I make the biggest impact.

My first experience with "at-risk" students began in the early 1970's. I graduated with my BS degree in 1972. Shortly after graduation, I began working as an instructional aid at a comprehensive high. I had a sincere interest in working with students who were struggling academically,

Dr. Paul A. Rodríguez & Dr. Roberto F. Casas

primarily Chicano gang youth. With this interest, I was recruited to begin teaching at a continuation high school in Alhambra, California suburb of Los Angeles.

It was then and is now my belief that public education should meet the needs and learning styles of <u>all</u> students, including those considered at-risk of dropping out. In reviewing the article, Alternative Curriculum Designs (Schubert, W. 1994), it is stated: "The guiding force of design resides in the minds, the perspectives and conceptualizations of those who teach, and those who develop policy for the what, how and why of teaching" (p. 26).

Furthermore, with the plethora of alternative delivery models such as Independent

Reflective Practices:
Perspectives of Multi-Unicultural School Leaders

Study, continuation high schools, opportunity classes, community day schools. Independent study is designed to offer personal learning experience where the pupil (student), parent and school jointly assume the responsibility for setting goals and activities. This model is intended to help students continue their education, where their own unique situations, such as medical problems, handicapped parents, or full-time work, necessitates their voluntary enrollment into independent study. This reform effect is designed to improve learning and instruction in our district. As stated above, the curriculum design for each student is a joint decision between the

Dr. Paul A. Rodríguez & Dr. Roberto F. Casas

student, parent and teacher based on the student's education plan. The Chino Valley Unified School District's independent study option is equivalent in quality and quantity to regular classroom instruction and enables students to complete the school district's adopted course of study within the customary period.

Students enrolled in independent study have access to the same services and resources available to other students, including the opportunity for students to be concurrently enrolled in elective courses at the comprehensive campus when those electives, resources, or programs are not readily available through the independent study program.

Reflective Practices:
Perspectives of Multi-Unicultural School
Leaders

To have students participant in their own personalized instruction helps them to internalize their own inner curriculum. Among the literature reviewed regarding curriculum development, Schubert stated (1997) Curriculum is made for students, but it is not of and by them." (p. 78)

Why use this approach?

The case approach is best for looking at independent study design because it is a sound approach for studying curriculum delivery. The content of this case study is based on my personal knowledge of supervising various independent study models in several districts and through interviews of students, parents and teachers involved in the dependent approach. I have also reviewed the various state mandates, district policy and the written curriculum agreements and student assignments that are part of this delivery model.

Demographics

The Chino Valley Unified School District is made up of <u>30</u> schools with a student enrollment of 31, 545 students. There are currently 300 students enrolled in independent study and 164 enrolled in Home Based education (home schooling). The demographics of the district are .2% American Indian or Alaska Native (60), 6.6% Asian (2,074), .3% Pacific Islander (101) 40.7% Hispanic/Latino (12,840), 5.2%

Reflective Practices:
Perspectives of Multi-Unicultural School
Leaders

African American (1,639), 3.3% Filipino (1,026), 43.8% White (not Hispanic) (13,805).

Definitions

I will be referring to several programs under my supervision that utilize the independent study model.

<u>*The Independent Study Program*</u> *is a specially designed program housed in classrooms located at each comprehensive high school campus.*

Students meet with teachers a minimum of one hour per week and are assigned twenty hours of "outer curriculum" per week. Typically, students will work on two to four subjects at any given time until completion of each subject matter. Students also have opportunities to participate in athletics, career counseling and club/school activities. Staff consists of seven teachers and six classified employees.

<u>Home Based Education</u> is a center located on a Junior High School Campus that serves families or students who are home schooled by their parents. The staff consists of six teachers and one counseling assistant. A counselor serves both programs and is itinerant.

<u>Critical Incidents</u>

Between 1992 until 1997 the independent

Reflective Practices:
Perspectives of Multi-Unicultural School
Leaders

study program was centralized at the continuation high school site, separated by several chain-linked fences and in several run-down portable classrooms. Only high school students were afforded the opportunity to enroll in the independent study program.

Students had to find their own way to the program and the books and materials were negligible to say the least. Students merely worked out of packets or discarded books or teacher made curriculum. There was not alignment with the district course of study or state standards.

However, on August 21, 1997, the school board voted on and ratified Board Policy

6158 (a-g), decentralizing the program and moving independent studies to each high school site and initiating the Home Based education program for elementary, middle-school and high school students.

By the fact that each of the three high school sites has their own program to serve the students from each high school area, has enabled students to be concurrently enrolled in independent study for their core course and several electives. Students can participate in extra and co-curricular activities at each school site.

In Board Policy 6158 (a) under section B: Limitations: #5 states:

"The district's independent study option shall be substantially equivalent in

Reflective Practices:
Perspectives of Multi-Unicultural School
Leaders

quality and quantity to classroom instruction, thus enabling students enrolled in independent study to complete the District's adopted course of study within the customary time frame. Students in independent study shall have access to the same services and resources as is available to other students in the school."
The concept and option of independent study is essential if schools are charged with meeting the needs of all students through equal access. In the article, Some Schools Work and More Can (Edmonds, R. R. 1979) the author stated:

> *"How many effective schools would you have to see to be*

persuaded of the educability of all children? If your answer is more than one, then I submit that you have reasons of your own for preferring to believe that basic pupil performance derives from the family background instead of school response to family background. Whether or not we will ever effectively teach the children of the poor is probably far more a matter of politics than of social science and that is as it should be." (p. 29)

Before 1997, students enrolled in independent study did not have many choices for elective courses, as did their counterparts at the comprehensive high school. At the present moment, students can now take the following courses as elective: Astronomy, Cartooning 1 and 2, Child Development 1 and 2, Consumer and Family Science 1 and 2, Contemporary Issues, Drawing and Painting 1 and 2, Drivers Education, Housing Interior and Design 1 and 2, Introduction to Art, Keyboarding 1 and 2, Word-processing, Single and Married Life, Law, Justice and You, Study Skills and World Geography. In addition, students can participate in clubs and groups at each campus.

Several other critical incidents helped shape the delivery of services to students enrolled in independent study. In the last three years, the program went from worksheet/workbook driven, to very few workbooks, to the use of state adopted textbooks. The texts used are regular textbooks, and basic workbooks as well as various supplemental materials.

Another critical incident that reformed the program was the creation of three different levels for each subject area in the core courses by the teachers in the program. The pre-assessment of each student is done to determine the academic level of each student. The staff uses several basic assessment instruments such as the "Brigance" for Math levels and the "Wide Range Achievement Test (WRAT)" for

Reflective Practices:
Perspectives of Multi-Unicultural School Leaders

reading levels.

An additional decision that helped enhance the current independent study program was the purchase and utilization of technology. Two years ago (1998) the district purchased computers and software as support to the curriculum. Another decision that supported the outer curriculum was the purchase of over one hundred (100) videotape titles for students to use as follow-up assignments and for projects in the community. The purchase and connection to the Internet enables students to use the "world" for research. As an example, when a student is working on an assignment in criminal law, the student has

Dr. Paul A. Rodríguez & Dr. Roberto F. Casas

access to the Indiana Law Library.

The general belief of staff, students and parents (as verified through interviews) is that having independent study centers at each high school site is better for the utilization of resources, transportation, and networking.

Educational research now offers teachers a number of processes that will increase the probability of student learning and achievement. Independent study is an effective delivery model for at-risk students. Effective implementation of the independent study option is essential to attain maximum benefit for students.

I have found through practice and through research that teachers of low achievers and or non-motivated students need to present information in a variety of ways and build into curriculum methods that students can use to process information.

The more actively involved low achievers and non-motivated students become in their learning, the greater the likelihood that it will have meaning, retention, and transfer. The goal of independent study is to help students through a personalized approach and for them to process information in meaningful ways in order to become independent learners. Goodlad (1984) stated:

> "If students are to learn, they must become engaged with subject

> matter, whether it is a mathematical problem, the characteristics of some other culture, the shaping of clay, or the structure of a poem. This engagement does not occur similarly for all kinds of learning; nor does it occur similarly for all individuals, whatever the subject matter. A concept needs to be read about, perhaps danced or acted out and eventually used in some meaningful content." (p. 35).

Critique of Reform Effort in Light of Reform Purposes

A brief overview of this case study is that

Reflective Practices:
Perspectives of Multi-Unicultural School
Leaders

up until 1997 the independent study delivery model was centralized and did not afford optimal learning for students. The former program created problems with student transportation, lack of access to the same services and resources as their counterparts at the regular high schools.

In 1997, the position of Director of Alternative Education and Programs was created. I held the position for the Chino Valley Unified School District. Since that time, there have been key personnel changes particularly at the policy making level (Superintendent, Board members) that enabled a paradigm shift in the organization, that places an emphasis on the concept that all students can learn. The paradigm shift requires the district to provide equal access to programs to all students. Thus, the change was made to decentralize and expand the independent study option for students, but maintained the expanded program in the current setting.

In the article Ten Curriculum Questions for Principals, (Schubert, W. H. 1991) the author stated: ". . . The most insightful state leaders and local administrators realize the complexity of the problem of curriculum design and know that effective planning must be done by those influenced by the planning." (p. 2)

Schubert W. H. (1991) indicated: " . . .

Reflective Practices:
Perspectives of Multi-Unicultural School Leaders

Curriculum planners must be aware of the diversity of interpretations of contemporary issues and they must entertain the possibility of new forms of teacher education, in-service education and teacher – learning situation." (p. 3)

The whole notion of meeting the needs of all students must also include a change in the mindsets of educators on how students learn and that one size fits all (i.e. regular high school), does not "fit all" students in their learning style.

As we continue to flesh out the thesis that "every student can learn" and that students shall have equal access to educational programs, we will soon begin to see not only that "all students can learn" but also that teachers will start coming to reality through education at-risk students, that the paradigm shift must now be, "I can teach all students."

If we are to have classrooms, and indeed, whole sites of classrooms that allow for different perspectives of teachers and learners, we will need to allow for more movement and self-direction by students, as we do in the independent study program.

In the final analysis, the entire hullabaloo about educational reform is beside the point when it comes to how people learn. It is not up to us adults to change this; the change is already there, in the faces in the

Reflective Practices:
Perspectives of Multi-Unicultural School
Leaders

classrooms. It is only up to us to decide if we will learn to keep pace with change, or choose to ignore it at the expense of students.

In putting educational program delivery in the proper perspective, meeting the needs of all learners will be a great challenge. However, with every challenge comes opportunities and with reform comes positive change and new ways of doing business. Curriculum design will be the vehicle that will enhance change.

In retrospect, reform efforts and the results of reform by its mere purpose must be driven by organizational change. However, there must be some benchmark values that stir change, such as efficacy principles and resiliency factors.

A good way to check if reform is effective is to utilize value inventories. Dr. Dale L. Brubaker references one such inventory in the book Creative Curriculum Leadership authored. The two-question instrument (p. 21) is labeled Appendix B An Organizational Change and Conservation Inventory. It asks the reader to identify what organization they work for or want to see change in, and are asked the following questions:

- *What are three things about your organization you highly value and want to continue? List.*

Reflective Practices:
Perspectives of Multi-Unicultural School
Leaders

- *What are three things about your organization that you want to change? List.*

Policies Changed

Regulatory: The policy and administrative regulations dealing with independent study were adopted August 21, 1997 and revised February 4, 1999 by the Chino Valley Unified School District, Board of Education The key component of verification of student work completion, advancement and progress is done through an independent study master agreement for each student and maintained on file along with completed corresponding work (attached). Also, as part of this policy and *administrative regulation is the permission to establish home schooling through independent study. Home Based education is the program that provides support for home-schooled families in the Chino Valley Unified School District.*

Educative: The educative policies relative to independent studies are:

- *Specially designed independent study classrooms at each high school*
- *Access to all programs at the comprehensive high school through concurrent enrollment*
- *Individualized work stations using computer assisted instruction*

***Reflective Practices:
Perspectives of Multi-Unicultural School
Leaders***

- *Classroom materials equal to those used by all students*
- *Opportunities for students to participate in athletics, career counseling and club activities*

Also, as part of the educative policies to the master agreement is the students' Individualized Learning Plan (ILP). The components of this plan are that each student will have an ILP that states:

- *The length of the agreement*
- *Statement of the objectives*
- *Method of evaluation*
- *Credits assigned*
- *The manner, time, frequency and place for submitting assignments*

Dr. Paul A. Rodríguez & Dr. Roberto F. Casas

<u>Summary, Conclusions, Recommendations</u>
Programmatic Recommendations: In this case study I spoke to the fact that Chino Valley Unified School District has restructured and has entered into a paradigm shift about the design and implementation of independent study delivery.

I hope that the reform of the independent study program will improve student achievement among students enrolled in the program. In an article entitled School Reform in the Information Age (Menlinger, H. 1996) the author stated: " . . . But the synergy of school restructuring, new forms of learning and teaching and technology will make the difference . . ." (p. 402)

***Reflective Practices:
Perspectives of Multi-Unicultural School
Leaders***

No learning environment or teaching strategy will work for all students, but research indicates that some have a higher probability of bringing about success with at-risk students in various types of delivery models. I suggest that these students be identified early during formative years and those social and academic interventions and enrichment programs be implemented. I have found that the key ingredient in successful programs for at-risk students is the attitude of the classroom teacher.

It is recommended that educational leaders utilize efficacy principles and resiliency factors when designing similar types of educational delivery models.

Dr. Paul A. Rodríguez & Dr. Roberto F. Casas

In the article, Why Aren't We Getting Along? (Gay, G., Slaughter, B., Baker, C. et al 1995), Holistic Education Review, it stated: "Getting along, interpersonally and interculturally is imperative for the well-being and betterment of both individuals and society." (p. 30)

It is my belief that by communicating high expectations, utilizing a variety of effective teaching strategies, and emphasizing the development of the total student, the teacher can be successful with students who are at-risk. Students enrolled in independent study have to be self-motivated to be successful. This is because much of their <u>outer</u> curriculum is completed at home, without the help of a

Reflective Practices:
Perspectives of Multi-Unicultural School
Leaders

teacher to mediate the students' progress. Among the literature I reviewed were several articles from Educational Leadership (April 1986): The author used the term, mediator to describe a teacher's role.

> *"As a mediator, the strategic teacher intercedes between the students and the learning environment to help students learn to grow, anticipates problems in learning and plans solutions to solve them, and guides and coaches students through the initial phase of learning to independent learning." (p. 5)*

Dr. Paul A. Rodríguez & Dr. Roberto F. Casas

With this in mind, the teacher involved in independent study program is the "key factor" in assisting at-risk students to be successful.

Recommendations for Further Study: It is my recommendation that the school district continue to offer a myriad of educational options to help all students to be successful. Independent study must continue to be assessed and audited in order to ensure that this educational option is meeting state mandates, but more importantly, is helping students in the Chino Valley Unified School District to meet their educational goals.

It is exciting to think that the day is coming when all students, whether from the affluent

Reflective Practices:
Perspectives of Multi-Unicultural School Leaders

part of our district, the barrio or the farming area, will have an equal educational opportunity. This is not an impossible vision. With the paradigm shift of our school board and the superintendent, together we can make it happen, through the development of educational options such as independent study.

Further study and research must continue relative to the design of educational delivery models. Consideration must be emphasized about the student's "inner curriculum" and experiences. Moreover, further study must continue relative to the improvement of "at-risk" student achievement with efficacy principles and *resiliency factors.*

Lastly, the review of independent study is relevant to the curriculum ideas I garnered from the lectures, readings and activities. The case study format revealed the direct impact on practice and the understanding on how curriculum decisions (both inner curriculum and outer curriculum are made and the effects on student achievement.

References

Adams, D. M., and Maine, E. W. 1998. Business ethics for the 21st century. Mountain View, CA: Mayfield Publishing.

Advisory Committee for the Public schools Accountability Act. (2000) Summary of Issues and Recommendations for the Development and Implementation of an Alternative Schools Accountability Model. The Public Schools Accountability Act (chapter3,statutes of 1999) Sacramento: Alternative accountability Subcommittee.

American Association of school Administrators Executive Committee. 1981. American Association of School Administrators.

Bennis, W. G. 1997. Managing people is like herding cats. Utah: Executive Excellence Publishing.

Blanchard, K., and Peale, N. V. 1998. The power of ethical management. New York: William Morrow.

Bolton, G. 2010. Reflective practice, writing and professional development, 3rd ed. California: SAGE Publications.

Boloz, S. 1997. "The C Diet" (unpublished manuscript). Shaping school culture: the heart of leadership. T. E. Deal. and K. D. Peterson, 17–18. San Francisco, CA: Jossy-Bass.

Boud D., Keogh R., and Walker D. 1985. Reflection, turning experience into learning. Routledge.

Brubaker, Dale L.1994. Creative Curriculum Leadership. Thousand Oaks, CA: Corwin Press Inc.

Casas, R. 1999. "Educational Leadership Appraisal, Final Project" (unpublished paper). National Ed.D. Program for Educational Leaders. Nova Southeastern University: Los Angeles, California.

Casas, R. & Rodriguez, P. 2012. *Reflective Practice of Multi-Unicultural school Leaders:* Strategies and Considerations for Improving Achievement of Cross-Culturally Diverse Students. Xlibris publications. ISBN: 978-1-4691-6294-2, Chino, CA.

Coleman, J.S., Campbell, E.Q., Hobson, C.J., McPartland, J., Mood, A.M., Weinfeld, F.D., & York, R.L. 1966. Equality of educational opportunity. Washington, D.C., US Dept. of Health, Education & Welfare. Office of Education.

Cubberly, E.P. 1909. *Changing Conceptions of Education:* Boston, Houghton Mifflin.

Daggett, W. R. and Kruse, B. 1997. Education is NOT a spectator sport. International Center for Leadership in Education: Schnectady, NY: Leadership Press.

Deal, T. E., and Peterson, K. D. 1999. Shaping school culture: the heart of leadership. San Francisco, CA: Jossey-Bass.

Drucker, Peter F. 2010. Graduate School of Management." Qualities of effective leadership: Principles of Peter F. Drucker. Lecturer: September 13, 2010.

Education Week. 2014. Resistance to Common Core Mounts. (Internet Magazine).

Edmond, R. R. 1979. "Some Schools Work and More Can." Social Policy 9, (March/April)

***Reflective Practices:
Perspectives of Multi-Unicultural School
Leaders***

Ellis, A. 2000. Educational Leadership Appraisal, Study Guide. National Ed.D. Program for Educational Leaders, Nova Southeastern University: Los Angeles, CA.

Franco, C.S.; Ott, M.G. and Robles, D.P. 2011. The Shaping of culturally proficient leaders, Leadership Magazine.

Freedman, S.W. (1993). Linking Large-Scale Assessment and Classroom Portfolio Assessment. Education Leadership, Vol.5, p.16-17.

Fullan, M. (1999), Change Forces: The Sequel, Journal of Educational Change.

Fullan, M. 2003. The moral imperative of school leadership. Thousand Oaks, CA: Sage Publications.

Gay, G., Slaughter, B., Baker, C.1995. "Why Aren't We Getting Along?" Holistic Review.

Goodlad, J. I. 1984. "Curriculum and Effective Teaching." In Perspectives on Effective Teaching and the Cooperative Classroom, edited by Judy Reinhartz, Washington, D.C., and National Education Association.

Green R. L. 2001. Practicing the arts of leadership. New Jersey: Prentice-Hall.

Greenberg, J., and Baron, R. A. 2000. Behavior in organizations, 7th ed. Upper Saddle River, NJ: Prentice Hall.

Griffiths, D. E. 1979. Another look at research on the behaviors of administrators. In G. L. Immegart and W. L. Boyd, Eds. Problem-finding in educational administration, 41–62. Lexington, MA: DC Heath.

Reflective Practices:
Perspectives of Multi-Unicultural School
Leaders

Heifetz, R. A. 1994. Leadership without easy answers. Cambridge, MA: Belknap/Harvard.

Heifetz, R., and Linsky, M. 2002. Leadership on the line: staying alive through the dangers of leading. Boston: Harvard Business School Press.

Hernandez, C. 2010. Personal communications. Lynwood, CA: Thurgood Marshall Elementary School.

House, R. J., Shane, S. A., and Herold, D. M. 1996. Rumors of the death of dispositional research are vastly exaggerated. Academy of Management Review.

Hoy, W. K., and Miskel, C. G. 1996. Educational administration: theory, research, and practice, 5th ed. New York: McGraw-Hill.

Jones, Beau F. (1986). "Quality and Equality through Cognitive Instruction." Educational Leadership, 44(7), (April 1986), p. 5-11.

Kennedy, M. 1994. The ownership project: An experiment in student equity. Social Studies Review 33(2), 24–30.

Kennedy, M. 1998. "More than a game: Eight transition lessons chess teaches." Reaching today's youth 2(4), 17–19.

Kirkpatrick, S. A., and Locke, E. A. 1991. "Leadership: Do traits matter?" Academy of Management Executive, 5, 48–60.

Larrivee, B. 2000. " Transforming Teaching Practice: Becoming the critically reflective teacher". Reflective practice 1.

Leitch, R., and Day, C. 2000. "Action research and reflective practice: Towards a holistic view". Educational action research 8, 179.

Lindsey, R. B., Nuri Robins, K., and Terrell, R. D. 2003. Cultural proficiency: A manual for school leaders, 2nd ed. Thousand Oaks, CA: Corwin.

Mehlinger, H. (1996). "School Reform in the Information Age." Phi Delta Kappan, (February, 1996), p. 400-407.

Monroe, L. 1997. Nothing's Impossible: Leadership lessons from inside and outside the classroom. New York, NY: Public Affairs.

Ott, J. S. 1989. The organizational culture perspective. Pacific Grove, CA: Brookes/Cole.

Osterman, K. F., Kottkamp, R. B. 1993. Reflective practice for educators: improving schooling through, professional development. Newbury Park, CA: Corwin Press.

Regional Equity Assistance Center (Region IX): Recommendations on the Implementation of the Common Core State Standards, (2013).

Reinhartz, J., and Beach, D. 2004. Educational leadership; changing schools, changing roles. Boston, MA: Allyn and Bacon.

Rodriguez, P. 2010. Personal communications. Montebello, CA: Vail HS.

Rodriguez, P (2013) Personal Interview, Pasadena, CA.

Schon, D. 1993. The reflective practitioner, how professionals think in action. Basic Books.

Schubert, W. H. (1991). "Ten Curriculum Questions for Principals." NASSP Bulletin, (February, 1991), p. 1-10.

Schubert, W. H. (1994). "Alternative Curriculum Designs." Curriculum on Teacher, 9, (1994), p. 26-31..

Schubert, W. H. (1997). "What is Citizenship and Who is J.D.? Educational Leadership, (October, 1997), p. 76-81.

Souza, D. (2004) <u>The Leadership Brain: How to Lead Today's Schools More Effectively. (p.69-78 The School Administrator.</u>

Vail High School. 2010. School Wide Action Plan. Montebello, CA.

Dr. Paul A. Rodríguez & Dr. Roberto F. Casas

Wallace Foundation. 2004. "Leadership Effectiveness Knowledge Foundation Committee Report" (draft). Unpublished document, 11. New York: Author. In J. Murphy, S. N. Elliott , E. Goldring and A. C. Porter, Learning-centered leadership: a conceptual foundation. Vanderbilt University.

ABOUT THE AUTHORS

Dr. Rodríguez is an educational leader focused on supporting local, state and national initiatives and programs. Dr. Rodriguez is a member of various educational organizations, including, the California League of High Schools and Association of California Administrators. Dr. Rodríguez has served on the California Awards for Performance Excellence California state as a senior examiner, Distinguished Schools, Schools to Watch, Gold Ribbon Awards and 21st Century imitative.

Dr. Rodríguez has been in the educational profession for over thirty-six years, having served as an elementary classroom teacher, high school counselor and high school principal in traditional and alternative

Dr. Paul A. Rodríguez & Dr. Roberto F. Casas

education.

Contact and visit Dr. Paul A. Rodriguez at:

par913@me.com

http://www.par913edu.com

http://www.california-commoncorestandards.com

Dr. Roberto F. Casas is the state chair for the administrative credential and graduate degree program for the five California campuses of Argosy University. He has served as an adjunct professor in graduate and undergraduate courses in education and educational leadership for Cambridge College, Chapman University, Ontario; Concordia University, Irvine; and California State University, Los Angeles. Dr. Casas retired from public education in 2008 after serving more than thirty-six years. He served as deputy superintendent for Lynwood Unified School District and as district superintendent for Brawley Union High School District in California. Dr. Casas retired as the associate dean for Pacific Oaks College in 2015. He served as a teacher, assistant principal, and principal for middle and high schools. He is a member of the Association of California School Administrators, Association of Latino Administrators and Superintendents, and California Association of Supervisors of Child Welfare and Attendance.

Dr. Paul A. Rodríguez & Dr. Roberto F. Casas

Before receiving his educational doctorate in educational leadership and organizational management from Nova Southeastern University, Dr. Casas earned his MA in educational administration and his BS in recreation/sports administration from California State University, Los Angeles. Dr. Casas can be contacted at: dr.casas53@yahoo.com

www.ingramcontent.com/pod-product-compliance
Lightning Source LLC
Chambersburg PA
CBHW041431300426
44115CB00001B/1